Miami for Families

UNIVERSITY PRESS OF FLORIDA

Florida A&M University, Tallahassee
Florida Atlantic University, Boca Raton
Florida Gulf Coast University, Ft. Myers
Florida International University, Miami
Florida State University, Tallahassee
New College of Florida, Sarasota
University of Central Florida, Orlando
University of Florida, Gainesville
University of North Florida, Jacksonville
University of South Florida, Tampa
University of West Florida, Pensacola

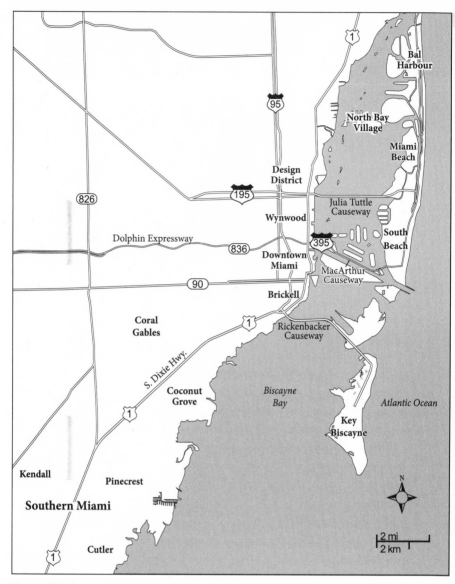

Greater Miami

MIAMI
for Families
A Vacation Guide for Parents and Kids

LAURA ALBRITTON

University Press of Florida

Gainesville · Tallahassee · Tampa · Boca Raton

Pensacola · Orlando · Miami · Jacksonville · Ft. Myers · Sarasota

A Florida Quincentennial Book

University Press of Florida
15 Northwest 15th Street
Gainesville, FL 32611-2079
http://www.upf.com

The activities in this book are meant to be fun and exciting for the entire
family. As in any situation, please use caution, obey all posted rules and
regulations, and use common sense. The publisher and the author are not
responsible for participation in any of these events or activities nor can
they be held liable for any possible injury.

Contents

Miami for Families

Running for a swim on Key Biscayne.
Photo by Laura Albritton.

Introduction

Situated on the tip of the Florida peninsula where the Atlantic Ocean's waters grow warm and inviting, Miami is an incredible tourist destination. This exotic locale enjoys some of the world's most beautiful beaches fringed with coconut palms and shady sea grape trees. Beyond the beaches, Miami offers everything from a classic marine park with dolphins to its world-famous Art Deco district. There are so many adventures waiting to be had. Your children can kayak with manatees off Key Biscayne, hand-feed macaws at Jungle Island, or ride a camel at Zoo Miami. Boating, standup paddleboarding, windsurfing, tennis, golf, and, of course, swimming are easily accessible. Whether you want to plunge into the clear waters of Coral Gables' Venetian Pool or the pedestrian-friendly hubbub of glamorous South Beach, Miami will surprise you with its wonderful variety.

Miami for Families: A Vacation Guide for Parents and Kids aims to make your family's vacation in Miami as fun, rewarding, and stress-free as possible. Every site, activity, and restaurant is selected with the particular needs of parents traveling with children in mind.

The chapters of this book divide Miami into eight manageable neighborhoods: "Key Biscayne"; "Coconut Grove"; "South Beach"; "Mid-Beach and Beyond"; "Coral Gables and Little Havana"; "Southern Miami"; "Downtown"; and "Wynwood and the Design District." Families can mix it up or focus their vacation on a particular area. At the end of the guidebook is a chapter entitled "Further Afield" that includes short trips to the Everglades, Key Largo, and Key West.

Activities and attractions are labeled by age, using designations B/T for Babies/Toddlers, M for children aged 4–9, TW for tweens aged 10–13, and TN for teenagers. Textboxes highlight important information: Deals, for great bargains; Splurges, for when you want to plan a special outing; Rainy Days, for indoor activities; Inside Scoops, for insider secrets from Miami residents; Survival Tips, on safety, health, and transportation concerns; and Necessities, for stores where you can purchase essentials.

Miami for Families is dedicated to the idea that a great family vacation is one in which both parents and their children enjoy themselves. Whether you are a family of six, a single parent of one, gay parents with twins, or grandparents who care for their grandchildren, you will find loads of ideas in this guidebook. Packed with insights and strategic advice, this book aims to be an invaluable tool in crafting a memorable vacation.

Practicalities

When to Visit

Any day, any time of year, can potentially be a warm, postcard-sunny day in Miami. If your family wants to luxuriate in true tropical heat, the summer season is the obvious time to visit. From May to September air temperatures rise to the high 80s and low 90s (30 to 35 Celsius). The water grows warm simultaneously, with the average ocean temperature in July at 86 degrees. Yet hurricane season is the mitigating factor. From June through October tropical thunderstorms are more likely to sweep through Florida, and some rain is to be expected. Although a direct hit by a hurricane is rare, during this season it is not a bad idea to purchase travel insurance.

The summer months of June, July, and August are considered low tourist season; shoulder season includes May, September, October, and November. During these months you're more likely to get a good deal on hotel and airfare. (Three exceptions are: the Miami Beach Urban Music Festival over Memorial Day weekend,

High Season	Shoulder Season	Low Season
December through April	May, September, October, and November	June, July, and August
Mild temperatures (60s to 80s) with cool "snaps"	Temperatures usually warm (70s to high 80s)	Warm (80s to 90s)
Dryer air, low humidity, less chance of rain	Good chance of tropical thunderstorms (Sept and Oct); moderate chance of showers (May and Nov)	Regular thunderstorms, often followed by bright sunshine; high humidity
High airfare and hotel prices	Moderate airfare and hotel prices	Some airfare and hotel deals to be found
More crowds, especially on Miami Beach	Fewer crowds, except for holiday weekends	Fewer crowds, except for holiday weekends

the Fourth of July weekend, and Labor Day weekend.) Because there is no time of year when tourists *don't* visit Miami, it usually pays to make your reservations well in advance.

During January, February, March, April, and December, crisp blue skies and a refreshing lack of humidity make these months prime tourist season; hotel rates and airfares increase, and in general tourist attractions become more crowded. Some visitors love the cooler weather: in January average daytime highs are in the 70s, while the sea temperature falls to 71 degrees.

Do you prefer the summer season in all its warm, tropical glory? Or will you and your children savor the city most in a crisper climate? Let your family's predilections and your own budgetary considerations guide your decision about the ideal time of year to vacation here.

What to Pack

In terms of practical necessities, Miami drugstores carry all mainstream brands of diapers and formula, but if your children need organic, hypo-allergenic, or otherwise specialty supplies, take them along. A small box of nonperishable snacks or crackers for your purse or knapsack can come in handy, too. Once in Miami, be sure to purchase bottled water or keep your reusable bottles filled; adults and children can become dehydrated faster than they realize in the heat. Carry a small bottle of high SPF (at least 30 to 40) sunscreen with you for that first morning or afternoon and then stock up on more after your arrival.

As far as clothes for the kids, for boys, shorts, shirts, a bathing suit, pair of jeans, pair of trousers, flip-flops, sneakers, and 1 nice pair of shoes should be sufficient. For girls, sundresses, shorts or skirts, jeans, shirts, swimsuits, a beach cover-up, sandals, flip-flops, and tennis shoes should cover all bases. Hats are a good idea for protecting noses and cheeks from the sun. For babies, bring outfits that will shield them from the sun's glare but not cling or bunch up in the heat. If your stroller has an attachable umbrella or shade, be sure to bring that, too. In the months of November, December, January, February, and March south Florida does experience the occasional cold snap; during those months, pack at least 1 set of warm layers for each member of the family.

As far as packing for the parents, you can't go wrong with good-looking resort wear. Miami adores its air-conditioning; even in summer it makes sense for women to pack a wrap or sweater and for men a jacket or blazer. Some travelers take a "When in Rome" approach on vacation and enjoy adapting their wardrobes to suit their destination. What if you're interested in dressing like a Miami local? In that case, keep in mind that residents cultivate a stylish, even flamboyant look, with body-conscious, colorful clothes. Women running around town wear flowy dresses and fashionable tunics and tops with slim-cut jeans, skirts, or dressy shorts. An attractive but comfortable pair of sandals or flats is priceless for day. At night, women here love their high heels. Chic cuff bracelets, statement necklaces, chandelier earrings, or hoops round out the Miami look. Miami men tend to favor dark-washed jeans, fitted trousers, and smart Bermuda shorts, paired with button-down or polo shirts. Weekend footwear for men translates into loafers, boots, leather flip-flops, and sandals. The city's sense of style carries over to the beach, where you'll see women of all ages and shapes wearing bikinis. Men wear trendy board shorts or midthigh bathing suits. Sunglasses in Miami aren't just a fashion accessory; when the sun is out in full force, they really become a necessity.

Safety

In Miami, there are loads of opportunities to go swimming, kayaking, paddleboarding, windsurfing, boating, and otherwise exploring what the area has to offer. Whatever the activity, our children's safety remains every parent's top priority. So let's take a moment to discuss a few issues that will be relevant to your Miami vacation. First, there's the subject of sun safety. To remain healthy and safe under south Florida's intense, vibrant sun requires 2 things: keeping hydrated and protecting your family's skin. Spending time in bright, hot sunlight causes people to sweat, and of course sweating then decreases the level of the body's hydration. Dehydration can creep up on you quickly in Miami and has serious health consequences. For that reason it is vital that both parents and children drink water and other liquids throughout the day. Keep bottles and containers close by and filled. As doctors always remind us: don't wait until you or your children feel thirsty to drink water.

Many health and pediatric organizations recommend that we stay out of the sun during the hottest part of the day (10:00 a.m. to 4:00 p.m.). While this may not be appealing advice, there are ways of protecting ourselves from the full brunt of cancer-causing UV rays. Umbrellas at the beach can provide helpful shade. High SPF, waterproof sunscreen is important but must be reapplied throughout the day (because even the best appear to be only water resistant). Sunglasses with UV ray protection help fend off damage to the eyes. Long-sleeve bathing shirts with UPF (Ultraviolet Protection Factor) fibers are often very effective at guarding children's arms and torsos. An umbrella or shade on your stroller can also make a huge difference. Monitoring how much sun exposure your family's getting and taking breaks from the sunshine, is a commonsense way to prevent sunburn. Besides the dangers of sun damage, a red, lobster-y sunburn can ruin your family's time and make lying down to sleep at night exceptionally painful.

Many tragic accidents are prevented every year when children wear life jackets while boating, kayaking, paddleboarding, and participating in other water sports. Even strong swimmers can get into trouble in the water: it only takes a child slipping off a paddleboard, knocking his or her head on the board, and falling into the water unconscious for a happy afternoon to turn into every parent's worst nightmare. Unfortunately, Florida leads the United States in boating and water-related deaths. The U.S. Coast Guard estimates that 90 percent of drownings in America could have been prevented had the victims been wearing life jackets. Florida takes these statistics quite seriously. The Florida Fish and Wildlife Commission now has a "Wear It Florida" campaign to convince boaters and people using water-sports equipment to wear life jackets. Every parent will make his or her own decision about this issue. This guidebook strongly recommends that parents have their children wear appropriately sized child life jackets when on any vessel (including paddleboards and kayaks). Children don't necessarily like wearing them, but kids usually don't recognize how many young lives have been saved by the simple act of taking this safety precaution.

Finally, let's talk about road safety. For more than one year running, Miami's drivers have been ranked the rudest in the United States. Driving is probably the least enjoyable aspect of visiting or living in this city. You will regularly see drivers not use turn signals, suddenly cut across lanes of traffic, run red lights in order to turn left, and otherwise drive recklessly and without concern for others. For those of us who don't enjoy kamikaze-like road conditions, the key is to keep your cool, pay close attention to cars in front of, beside, and behind you, and avoid spending large blocks of time on the highways, if possible. Don't expect all of your fellow drivers to follow the rules; expect the unexpected. Try to schedule plenty of nondriving time during your vacation. In some neighborhoods, you can walk to attractions and restaurants.

Low tide and a calm sea at Hobie Beach on Virginia Key.
Photo by Laura Albritton.

However, because there is some lousy driving in Miami, pedestrians also need to take special care. That means when crossing the street, look carefully and look twice. Don't assume that a car will stop if the light turns red; make sure it does stop. If you have a crosswalk signal that says you can walk, continue to watch the road to ensure that drivers actually halt. Miami is not the worst U.S. city for pedestrians, but it is among the worst. Keep a close watch on young children especially. If you and your children decide to bike, be very cautious. Many drivers appear oblivious to cyclists' safety. Wearing bright colors is a good idea, as is choosing your biking route thoughtfully.

Safety concerns shouldn't overshadow your vacation. Most trips to Miami are, happily, accident-free. Precautions for sun, water, and road safety don't need to become a burden. Sunblock, good hydration, life jackets, and caution on the streets are easy to incorporate into your day, so you can move on and get to good stuff: adventures and relaxation with your kids.

Transportation

Most visitors who want to see sights throughout the city will do so by car. Car rentals are available at the Miami Airport's new Rental Car Center (RCC) in the Miami Intermodal Center; a "people mover" gets you quickly from the airport terminal to the facility. Major companies here include Alamo, Avis, Budget, Dollar, Enterprise, Hertz, Sixt, Thrifty, and others.

Alamo, 1.800.327.9633, http://www.alamo.com
Avis, 1.800.331.1212, http://www.avis.com
Budget, 1.800.527.0700, http://www.budget.com
Dollar, 1.800.4000, http://www.dollar.com
Enterprise, 1.800.325.8007, http://www.enterprise.com
Hertz, 1.800.654.3131, http://www.hertz.com
National, 1.800.227.7368, http://www.nationalcar.com
Sixt, 1.888.749.8227, http://www.sixt.com
Thrifty, 1.800.367.2277, http://www.thrifty.com

There are also rental offices in other locations such as Coral Gables (Hertz and Avis) and South Beach (Avis and Enterprise). If you plan to rent, and need a child's car seat, be sure to request it in advance.

Miami has public transportation, but it's not always convenient. Intrepid travelers use the bus system or the elevated Metrorail. The new Metrorail extension (Airport Link) connects the Metrorail to the Miami airport; if you are staying on the mainland (not Miami Beach) you may be able to use this public elevated rail system to get close to your hotel. Only the Orange line, which runs to the Dadeland South station in Kendall, connects to the MIA (Miami International Airport) station. If you need to go north of Earlington Heights, take the Orange line from the airport to the Earlington Heights station, then transfer to the Green line to head north. Leaving the airport, the Orange line Metrorail runs east and south to the following stations: Earlington Heights, Allapattah, Santa Clara, Civic Center, Culmer, Historic Overtown/Lyric Theater, Government Center, Brickell, Vizcaya, Coconut Grove, Douglas Road, University, South Miami, Dadeland North, and Dadeland South. Once you arrive at your Metrorail station, in most cases you will need to get a taxi or a bus to reach your hotel. (Super Yellow Cab 305.888.7777 or AAA Taxi 305.999.9990) It's not advisable to use this system late at night, when the train will deposit you and your children at a possibly empty station where you might wait a long while before a taxi comes. If you've just arrived in Miami for the very first time, using the Metrorail (plus bus or taxi) to go from airport to hotel could take more time and patience than you have to spare.

There is an express bus, the Airport Flyer, which takes you from the airport to Miami Beach for $2.35 per person; once on the beach, it makes only 3 stops (2 at 41st Street in Mid-Beach and 1 at Lincoln Road in South Beach). The fare for regular city buses is $2, although shorter shuttle bus routes cost only 25¢. If you're on a tight budget, you'll find that buses making neighborhood "loops" are the most straightforward to use.

Key Biscayne, due to its relatively small size, could be navigated using taxis along with city bus 102 (Route B), which travels to a downtown Miami Metrorail stop (Government Center), the Brickell Metrorail stop, then on Key Biscayne itself: the Rickenbacker Causeway, Miami Seaquarium, Crandon Beach Park, the Village of Key Biscayne, and Bill Baggs State Park. In Coconut Grove, the Coconut Grove Circulator (Route 249) is a shuttle that costs 25¢ per person and loops past Grand Avenue and Mc-Farlane Road, where shops, restaurants, and hotels are located, over to City Hall, and then to the Coconut Grove Metrorail station, from which you can travel to Brickell and Downtown. (The Metrorail fare is $2 per person.) The "Coconut Grove" chapter contains more information. The free Coral Gables Trolley travels from 8th Street (Calle Ocho) through the center of the Gables to U.S. 1 and the Douglas Street Metrorail station; it is of limited use to tourists but it does cut across the neighborhood if you want an overview. The trolley only runs on weekdays. The new Biscayne-Brickell Trolley is an absolutely free bus that travels from the Brickell neighborhood through Downtown. Making stops every 15 minutes, the trolley provides a convenient sightseeing tool for visitors staying in Downtown; it links to the Metrorail, too. See the "Downtown" chapter for more information.

For those who'd rather not drive at all, South Beach offers the most to do in a reasonably walkable neighborhood. Using the inexpensive shuttle bus and taxis is not difficult. You can also take a taxi from the airport to South Beach, or take the express Airport Flyer that makes limited stops on Miami Beach. In the "South Beach" chapter, transportation options are described in more detail.

Pricing

Hotel rates, the price of restaurant entrées, and entrance fees go up as inevitably as helium balloons rise in the sky. As a result, the rates quoted in any guidebook become out-of-date almost from the moment of publication. So please consider the specific prices listed in each chapter as general guidelines. Also, bear in mind that the hotel rates listed here represent the lowest found online using a variety of websites (hotel sites http://www.

kayak.com, http://www.booking.com, http://www.hotwire.com, http://www.hotels.com, http://www.expedia.com, etc.). Even when fees have increased, you can still use the figures in the book as a basis of comparison between properties.

Internet Extras

Connect with the author of this guidebook at http://www.miami forfamilies.com. This website is upbeat, family oriented, and monitored for child-appropriate content. Here you'll find information about seasonal events and more photographs of beautiful Miami.

On Facebook, check out the page Miami for Families! The author will post snapshots and updates about current happenings. Readers can add their comments and even family pictures of Miami activities. And, on Pinterest, take a look at enticing images of Miami, suggestions for your vacation wardrobe, and new locales on the Miami for Families boards. Hope to see you online!

A Brief History of Miami

From approximately 1200 to the early 1800s the Tequesta Indians inhabited the region that encompasses today's Miami, with their main village established at the mouth of the Miami River. They fished and hunted the abundant ocean, rivers, and forests. In 1513, Spanish explorer Juan Ponce de León sailed into Biscayne Bay and identified it as "Chequescha," but it's not known whether he made landfall. Fifty-four years later, Spanish Jesuit priests established a mission in the area to spread Catholicism. Tragically, the Spaniards brought with them European diseases such as smallpox, to which the Tequesta had no immunity. The consequence of disease and warfare was the near obliteration of the Tequesta by the 1750s. Today, the excavated Miami Circle in Downtown is one of the only reminders of this Florida tribe. Meanwhile, in the 1700s another tribe, the Seminoles, gradually formed in Florida from surviving members of various tribes, Creek Indians from Georgia, and a few runaway slaves.

Except for a brief period of English rule, Florida remained a colony of Spain until 1821, when Spain signed a treaty giving the territory to the United States. Settlers arrived to claim land grants from the government from 1800 onward, but the Miami area continued to be very sparsely populated. Due to dangerous reefs and tropical storms, ships wrecked off the coast, and soon wreckers arrived from Key West and the Bahamas to salvage the vessels. As a result of the nautical dangers the Cape Florida Lighthouse was constructed on Key Biscayne in 1825 by the U.S. government. In 1838 Fort Dallas was created as an outpost during the Seminole Wars. The area was sometimes called "Fort Dallas," and it also became known as the "Village of Miami" after the Miami River (whose name allegedly derived from the Mayaimi Indians of Lake Okeechobee). During this period of intermittent warfare (which ended in 1858) some Seminoles pushed deeper and deeper into the Everglades in order to avoid being seized by U.S. troops and forcibly removed from Florida.

In the 1880s and 1890s black Bahamians arrived to work at the new hotels, including Charles and Isabella Peacock's Bay View House, later the Peacock Inn (now the site of Coconut Grove's Peacock Park). The new Bahamian neighborhood was called Kebo, today Village West. Visionaries such as Ralph Middleton Munroe, Flora McFarlane, and writer Kirk Munroe purchased land in Coconut Grove and became full-time residents. Munroe's house, the Barnacle, is the oldest surviving home in Miami and is now open to the public within a state park.

Settlers such as William Brickell and Julia Tuttle also bought land and braved the wilderness. William and Mary Brickell ran a post office and trading post on the Miami River that served both the whites and the Seminoles, who arrived in canoes. Today "Brickell" is a waterfront neighborhood of high-rises south of Downtown, while the Julia Tuttle Causeway connects Miami to Mid-Miami Beach. It was Julia Tuttle who talked industrialist Henry Flagler into bringing his railroad down to Miami, which as of 1896 connected the area with the rest of the country.

The year 1896 was momentous for another reason: Miami was finally incorporated as a city. In the next 2 decades, the city's expansion took off at a delirious rate. Biscayne Bay was dredged to create a much larger Miami Beach, parts of the Everglades were drained, and so the emergence of Miami as a destination

83

North bank of the Miami River as seen from
Gilbert's Wharf, 1884. Photo by Ralph Middleton
Munroe. Courtesy of HistoryMiami.

for fun, sun, and good times—especially during Prohibition—began. John Collins (for whom Collins Avenue in South Beach is named) convinced others of the need for a bridge to connect Miami to Miami Beach and along with Carl Fisher bankrolled the project; the bridge opened in 1913. Up to this point, much of Miami Beach was mangrove swamp, untamed jungle, or the leftovers of failed coconut plantations. Brothers J. E. and J. N. Lummus began to develop their property here; along with Carl Fisher they paid for dredging to fill the land. Fisher even imported 2 elephants to help clear the stubborn indigenous undergrowth. Today Lummus Park in South Beach and Fisher Island memorialize their transformative efforts. Right from the very beginning, Miami was a place where dreamers and tycoons felt compelled to imprint their visions onto the Florida landscape.

A housing and land boom exploded in Miami in the 1920s. Developers, entrepreneurs, and ordinary people scrambled to buy land and build homes, which in turn led to an unsustainable increase in prices. Part of the appeal, besides the weather, was the lure of gambling and the widespread flouting of Prohibition. With every boom comes a bust, and the city was no exception. By 1925, the fever for real estate transformed into a chill. In 1926 the Great Miami Hurricane compounded the effects of the downturn, with tens of thousands of people left homeless and hundreds dead. When the Great Depression seized the country in 1929, the city was already hurting economically. But Miami never let calamity get it down for long.

As the 1930s got under way, architects and businessmen erected glorious Art Deco hotels on Miami Beach. These fanciful buildings, some with a nautical flair, put a new and original spin on the Art Deco movement and were destined to become one of the city's greatest treasures. When the United States entered World War II, Miami became an important strategic location, particularly with German submarines patrolling offshore. One Nazi sub was even sunk just near Miami Beach. With the U.S. Army and Navy moving into town, the once slumping fortunes of the area were reversed. By the end of the war, Miami's economy was once again humming along. "MiMo" or Miami Modern architecture emerged in the late 1940s, a style that married tropical glamour with modernism and reflected the area's optimism.

The next major transformation came in 1959, when Fidel Castro ousted Fulgencio Batista from the nearby island of Cuba. Overnight, Batista supporters fled the revolutionaries for Miami. As Castro's new government grew more overt in its embrace of communism, wealthy Cubans, particularly land- and factory owners, left in a wave known as the Golden Exile. After the Bay of Pigs invasion failed in 1961, many Cuban exiles in south Florida never forgave President Kennedy and switched their allegiance to the Republican Party. Middle-class Cubans also left the island for Miami. The profound demographic change resulted in a population that was increasingly Hispanic and Spanish-speaking, a development still very much in evidence today.

The 1970s and 1980s saw racial tensions boil over. Haitian refugees, sometimes pejoratively labeled "boat people" in the press, made the dangerous journey to south Florida often in unsafe vessels to escape political repression and poverty on Haiti. Because Haitians did not benefit from the same privileged legal status as Cubans, many Haitians were repatriated to their island, despite the fact that it was ruled by notorious dictator "Baby Doc" Duvalier. In Miami, Little Haiti grew into a thriving community, yet the suspicion among Haitians that they were treated differently from Cuban immigrants—for racial reasons—persisted. In late 1979, 4 white police officers were suspended for allegedly beating to death an African-American insurance agent, Arthur McDuffie. Their trial was moved to Tampa, where an all-white jury acquitted the officers. The subsequent riots rocked Miami, from historically black neighborhoods such as Overtown and Liberty City to Coconut Grove. Several were left dead. Eventually, Dade County paid McDuffie's family a civil settlement.

In 1980, Castro suddenly allowed Cubans to leave the island in private vessels. In a few months almost 125,000 Cuban refugees arrived in Miami in what was known as the Mariel boatlift. Although the vast majority of people who arrived during Mariel were law abiding, Castro deliberately expelled those considered "undesirables." Some of these people had faced persecution by the communist regime (homosexuals such as the poet Reinaldo Arenas, political dissidents, and people with mental illness) while a minority were common criminals. Despite the fact that only a small percentage of the refugees had a criminal background, unfortunately, Cubans who came during this period were sometimes wrongly associated with criminality. The misunderstanding resulted in paranoia and prejudice in Miami when it came to the newcomers.

In the 1980s huge amounts of South American cocaine were moved into the United States through Miami, which created a blistering crime wave. The TV show *Miami Vice* reflected the amount of drug money flowing into the local economy and the corruption and violence that came with it. In the decade that followed, the city had to grapple with the effects of Hurricane Andrew in 1992, a Category 5 storm that devastated swaths of housing and infrastructure and left 44 people dead. In the later 1990s the city staggered from financial troubles, with Miami's debt rating in 1996 reduced to junk bond status. The next century did not look promising when the Elian Gonzalez case inflamed old ethnic rivalries in 2000; Miami Cubans were pitted against their own relatives in Cuba, who advocated for the 6-year-old to be returned to his father. Many in the "Anglo" (non-Hispanic white) and African-American communities disagreed with the exiles' point of view. It looked like unrest might once again take over the streets, but somehow the city pulled through with protests but no loss of life.

In the past years, Miami has experienced continued growth. In general crime has dramatically decreased. Downtown has become a world-class center of commerce and would be unrecognizable to early settlers William Brickell and Julia Tuttle. Another real estate bust, this time global in nature, seemed to bring Miami's energetic market to its knees in 2008 but not permanently. An inflow of new arrivals and new money, this time in part from Brazil, started to revive its prospects.

Throughout its history, Miamians have been feverishly impatient for progress. As a result, few markers of the past remain, except for the odd church, house, or bridge that's escaped the ravenous hunger for the new. The urge to develop and expand collides with the need to preserve a bit of the past—putting pressure on even protected districts such as South Beach. The metropolis has always had a dual identity: as a mecca for pleasure-seekers and as a border town for immigrants. This duality creates a tension and a unique energy within the city. The one civic constant is restlessness.

In the last decade, Miami has reinvented itself as one of the most important art capitals in the United States, with significant galleries, major private collections, intriguing small museums, and an international art fair— Art Basel Miami Beach—that gets more successful every year. The opening of the Perez Art Museum Miami (PAMM) on Biscayne Bay highlights the city's artistic maturity. As a result of the changes, Miami has grown into a more interesting, culturally stimulating, and cosmopolitan city than ever before. With its beaches, tourist attractions, art, sports, and culture, it is no wonder that the city has become one of the most popular vacation destinations in the world.

Further Reading

For an entertaining overview of its history, read *Miami, U.S.A.*, a classic written by longtime resident Helen Muir. *Miami Then and Now* by Carolyn Klepser and Arva Moore Parks showcases gorgeous early photographs of the city, along with later images of its development. For portraits of Miami in specific eras, read the incisive but dark *Miami* by Joan Didion and David Rieff's excellent book *The Exile*. Edna Buchanan's Britt Montero mysteries focus on the seamy side of Miami. Cuban Miami is brilliantly portrayed in Cristina Garcia's *Dreaming in Cuban* and *The Aguero Sisters* and Ana Menendez's *In Cuba I Was a German Shepherd*. Contemporary Miami is explored in Patricia Engel's edgy short story collection *Vida*. Susanna Daniel's novel *Stiltsville* unfolds in 1969, against the backdrop of Biscayne Bay and the stilt houses that stand precariously in the open water. Daniel's recent novel *Sea Creatures* takes place in 1992, the year Hurricane Andrew struck the city, and is a gripping, beautifully rendered story.

Unfortunately, Tom Wolfe's recent Miami novel, *Back to Blood*, is marred by unbelievable characters and tired clichés. For excellent homegrown satire about the city, get Dave Barry's hilarious *Big Trouble* and *Insane City* and Carl Hiaasen's *Bad Monkey* and his classic *Tourist Season*. Children may enjoy reading Hiaasen's children's novel *Hoot*, set at a middle school in Coconut Grove and involving an effort to save miniature owls from the machinations of developers—an "only in Miami" kind of story. Finally, the *Miami Herald* and the weekly *Miami New Times*—and their websites—are matchless resources for what is happening in Miami.

Key Biscayne

A few miles off the mainland of Miami lies the beautiful island refuge of Key Biscayne. Palm trees, miles of beach, and seriously spectacular views make this a destination that some vacationers never want to leave. In fact, what many people call Key Biscayne is actually 2 small islands connected by causeways and bridges, Virginia Key and the Village of Key Biscayne. With a land mass of not quite one-and-a-half square miles, the Village of Key Biscayne itself is one of the most exclusive residential areas in the United States. Million-dollar condominiums, strictly enforced speed limits, and gorgeous waterfront make this one of Miami's most sought-after neighborhoods. But don't be put off by the steep real estate. Key Biscayne is one of Miami's great bargains for a family sun-soaked afternoon. For the modest $1.75 Rickenbacker Causeway toll you can enjoy free parking at beaches, or for a very reasonably priced entrance fee you can spend an entire day at one of Florida's best beach parks, Bill Baggs Cape Florida. What's more, Key Biscayne is very convenient to Coconut Grove, Brickell, South Beach, Downtown, and Coral Gables.

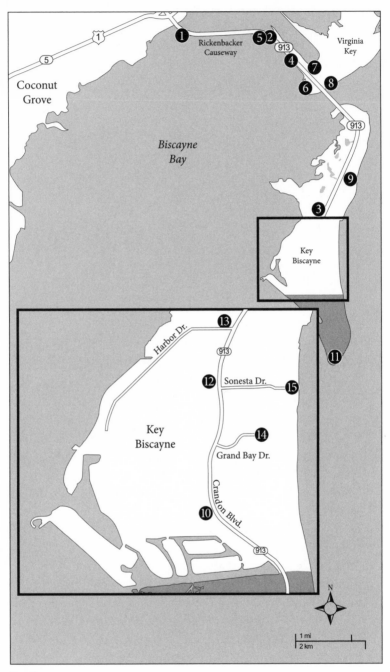

Key Biscayne

Working on a sand sculpture at one of Key Biscayne's family-friendly beaches. Photo by Zickie Allgrove.

The islands, which are connected to Miami by the 4-mile-long Rickenbacker Causeway, first became famous as the location of President Richard Nixon's "Winter White House." But the key's history extends to the early 19th century. In 1825 the U.S. government allocated funds to construct a 65-foot lighthouse at Cape Florida, the very tip of the uninhabited Key Biscayne. A schooner from the Northeast sailed in the bricks to build it. The light guided ships clear of the Florida Reef, which for years had proved deadly for unlucky vessels and sailors. In 1836 during the Second Seminole War, Seminoles attacked the lighthouse and the keeper's cottage. The assistant keeper, John Thompson,

Map Key

1. Rickenbacker Causeway
2. William Powell Bridge
3. Key Biscayne Tennis Association
4. Hobie Island Beach
5. Sailboards Miami
6. Miami Seaquarium
7. Virginia Key Beach and Picnic Area
8. Historic Virginia Key Beach Park
9. Crandon Beach Park
10. CVS Drug Store
11. Bill Baggs Cape Florida State Park
12. Forno e Fornelli
13. Oasis Café
14. The Ritz-Carlton Key Biscayne
15. Silver Sands Beach Resort

survived being shot, but his helper, African-American Aaron Carter, died as the lighthouse burned to the ground. The structure was rebuilt 10 years later, in 1846.

Today, the Cape Florida Lighthouse flourishes as a tourist attraction, and the fiercest battles raging on the key are over which government department will pay to repair a short bridge span. Key Biscayne enjoys a reputation as a magnet for sun enthusiasts, nature lovers, and tennis aficionados. In this relatively small section of Miami your family can enjoy everything from a marine park with a killer whale and dolphins to sit-on-the-edge-of-your-seat tennis.

The annual Sony Open in March hosts the greatest tennis stars, including Novak Djokovic, Serena Williams, Andy Murray, and Maria Sharapova. To attend this event you need to buy tickets in advance (http://www.sonyopentennis.com). Even if your visit doesn't coincide with the tournament, your family can still reserve a court on Key Biscayne or contact them to arrange a lesson with one of their pros.

Key Biscayne Tennis Association
6702 Crandon Blvd.
Key Biscayne 33149
305.361.5263
http://www.tenniskeybiscayne.com
Monday through Friday 8:00 a.m. to 9:00 p.m., Saturday and Sunday 8:00 a.m. to 6:00 p.m.
Ages: M, TW, TN

Before you reach Key Biscayne proper, you will drive onto the Rickenbacker Causeway and cross the William Powell Bridge, and then descend onto Hobie Island Beach. These beaches, which are in fact part of Virginia Key, have free parking. Before and after you reach the bridge there are vendors that rent kayaks, windsurfing equipment, and standup paddleboards (SUPs). For children old enough to paddle a kayak or paddleboard, or try wind- or kite-surfing, you don't have to go very far on the causeway to have a great time. One of the most dramatic views in Miami can be experienced while kayaking under the soaring William Powell Bridge, where graceful cormorants, ahningas, pelicans, and other waterbirds swoop into the ocean for fish. In winter months, manatees congregate in the waters off of Key Biscayne. These gentle aquatic mammals, grey in color with an average weight of 1,200 pounds, are a delight to watch from a kayak. (Don't attempt to touch them or intercept them, however; this is against the law.) Ask the staff where you rent equipment if manatees, dolphins, or other sea creatures have been spotted that day.

The Hobie beaches (after you cross William Powell Bridge) tend to be narrow strips of sand. The grounds and facilities have been upgraded in recent years, with new dune grasses and palm trees taking root. The usually shallow, bathtublike ocean conditions of this portion of Biscayne Bay make it easygoing for infants and toddlers. In fact, some young children prefer playing here to larger Key Biscayne beach parks that charge an entrance fee. Hobie Island is also one of the only dog-friendly beaches in Miami, and in general it's less developed than other locations (with fewer restrooms). Little children may occasionally find prickly bottle caps; there are no lifeguards on duty. If your family isn't interested in renting water-sports equipment, or if you are looking for wider stretches of sand, keep driving. These lie just a few minutes ahead.

Hobie Island Beach Park
Rickenbacker Causeway, Key Biscayne
Restrooms, fishing allowed, free parking
Limited concessions (ice cream, snacks)
Ages: B/T, M, TW, TN

There are various equipment rental vendors along Rickenbacker Causeway, notably 1 before and 2 after you cross William Powell Bridge. For typical rates, visit http://www.sailboards miami.com. Sailboards Miami is located on the right side of the causeway, just before you cross William Powell Bridge, at GPS coordinates N25.74569° W80.192368. Single kayaks cost $15 an hour and double kayaks are $20 an hour. Equipment for standup paddleboarding (SUP) costs $30 an hour. Children as young as 8 can try out a short-sized paddleboard, if water conditions are calm; children must wear life jackets and should stay close to shore. Sailboards Miami rents windsurfing and kiteboarding gear, too, and gives lessons. Visit their website or call 305.892.8992 for more information; you can also call to check conditions out on the water. Sailboards Miami opens at 10:00 a.m. and closes at 6:00 p.m., Fridays through Wednesdays.

Another company, Miami Catamarans, is situated on the right immediately after you cross the William Powell Bridge; teenagers and 'tweens may enjoy taking a sailing lesson or renting one of their Hobie Cats. Their website is http://www.miamicatamarans. com and their phone is 305.345.4104. A third company, Lubo's Place, rents paddleboards, pedal boats, beach chairs, and umbrellas. After you cross Powell Bridge, and then pass the Miami Catamarans rentals, look for the next rental location (with helpful flags) on the right before you reach Seaquarium. Lubo's Place is open 7 days a week; their website is http://www.standuppaddlekeybiscayne.com and their phone number is 786.301.3557. They also offer guided tours and SUP lessons. All 3 rental companies accept credit cards and cash for payment.

⊘ SURVIVAL TIP

Some water-sports companies will require children to wear life jackets; others will recommend it. Because even strong swimmers do go overboard and have accidents, this guidebook urges parents to keep children in life jackets while boating, kayaking, paddleboarding, and using other water-sports equipment. Every year in Florida the use of life jackets saves lives. For more on this issue, see the Safety section in the "Practicalities" chapter.

The first major land mass you'll encounter driving across Rickenbacker Causeway is Virginia Key. This prime beachfront real estate is home to the University of Miami's Rosenstiel School of Marine and Atmospheric Science. With both undergraduate and graduate programs, RSMAS researchers investigate the environment and climate; sustainable aquaculture and fisheries; coastal ecosystems; tropical cyclone tracking; and a host of other genuinely fascinating subjects. Virginia Key has been a family-friendly destination since 1955, when Miami Seaquarium opened as one of America's first marine-themed parks. On the other side of the causeway from Seaquarium is the turn-off for Virginia Key Beach, a low-key place to escape urban commotion.

The most prominent attraction on Virginia Key is, without a doubt, Miami Seaquarium. This old-school marine park also serves as a rehabilitation center for injured and orphaned manatees. Particularly geared for younger children, Seaquarium is a local Miami favorite. While it may not have the acreage, flash, or super-slick facilities of Orlando's theme parks, this institution has been working to reinvent and update itself. Recent additions include the new Sting Ray Touch Pool, where children can pet sting rays; Sharky's Sky Trail, a climbing adventure course; Sea Trek Reef Encounter, with participants walking inside a giant tropical aquarium; and Dolphin Harbour, where guests can interact with dolphins in the water.

The general entrance price to Seaquarium gives you access to its exhibits and shows. Exhibits include live sharks, seals, sea lions, manatees, tropical fish, sting rays, sea turtles, and parrots. One exhibit, Discovery Bay, showcases Florida wildlife and ecology, including several fearsome-looking alligators. At the manatee exhibit, you can watch caretakers feed manatees lettuce and apples. There are also regularly scheduled performance shows throughout the day with animals and their trainers. Top Deck Dolphin highlights the acrobatic ability of these remarkable mammals, while Golden Dome Sea Lion is a fun comedy show showcasing Salty the Sea Lion and his Reef Rangers (that is, seals). Flipper Dolphin highlights the latest TV Flipper, with friends, in a show set to beach music. Lolita and her dolphin pals show off their amazing moves in the Killer Whale and Dolphin show. These attractions will keep children busy for hours.

The delightful Top Deck Dolphin Show at Miami Seaquarium.
Photo by Zickie Allgrove.

For hefty extra fees, you can participate in a Dolphin Odyssey, Dolphin Encounter, Sea Trek Reef Encounter, the VIP Tour, or Trainer for a day. There are age restrictions for each activity, and reservations should be made in advance. Full details are on the Seaquarium website (http://www.miamiseaquarium.com). Strollers and wheelchairs are available for rent. There are snack bars and restrooms throughout the grounds. In terms of dining, Seaquarium offers the typical theme park menus (burgers, pizza, popcorn) with a few healthy options such as salads and grilled chicken. The gift shop sells cheerful stuffed whale and dolphin toys, along with other goodies designed to entice children.

Miami Seaquarium
4400 Rickenbacker Causeway
Key Biscayne 33149
305.361.5705
http://www.miamiseaquarium.com
Adults $39.95, children 3–9 years $29.95
Parking $8
9:30 a.m. to 6:30 p.m., 365 days a year (box office closes at 4:30 p.m.)
Ages: B/T, M, TW
*Teens will most enjoy the extra-fee animal encounters.

🌞 DEAL

If you plan to visit Miami twice in one year and want to return to Seaquarium, the annual pass at $54.95 per adult and $44.95 per child (3–9 years) can be a smart buy. It is also worth searching the internet for Seaquarium coupons before you visit. Often you will need to print these out, so make sure you check while you have access to a printer.

There are, somewhat confusingly, 2 different beaches known as "Virginia Key Beach." The first, Virginia Key Beach and Picnic Area, is located on Rickenbacker Causeway, on the left, just before you reach Seaquarium; there's a turn lane but no traffic light. After you enter and pay the $6 fee ($8 on weekends), you'll see a string of 4 parking lots on your right. From here, there is a 5- to 10-minute walk through the preserved South Florida "hammock" (forest). Suddenly, as you tramp down the dirt path, it seems like you've left metropolitan Miami behind and discovered a wild sanctuary for mangroves and tropical brush. You'll emerge right on the sand, ready to plunge into the clear, temperate waters. On this section of beach there are no public bathrooms or lifeguards. Sometimes, for reasons unannounced, these parking lots are closed. If that occurs or if you prefer access to restrooms, drive further down the road, where there is a more developed area with lifeguard stand, tiki huts, bathrooms, a volleyball court, playground, and extensive parking, directly on the beach.

The next Virginia Key Beach is Historic Virginia Key Beach Park, with an entrance on Rickenbacker Causeway, just *past* Seaquarium; there is a traffic light to indicate where you make a left. Before we venture on to a description, it's important to point out that NOAA, the National Oceanic and Atmospheric Administration, conducted a study here that revealed dangerous currents and a sudden drop-off not far from shore. A large sign announces No Swimming Allowed (but not the reasons for this), and so unwitting visitors continue to swim, while no one appears to stop them. As a result, the historic beach park isn't a good choice for a family afternoon, unless your family does *not* want to enter the water.

There is talk of creating "groins" or rock barriers to diminish the currents at this beach, so people can actually use the

The mini train at Historic Virginia Key Beach Park. Unfortunately, a study found dangerous currents off this beach. Photo by Zickie Allgrove.

park; this would be nice, since the place has an interesting history. This beach originated in 1945 when it was designated as Miami's segregated beach for African-Americans. Back then, in that era of unapologetic prejudice, the ocean of Miami Beach was strictly off-limits to the city's black residents. Once segregation ended, the beach on Virginia Key gradually fell into obscurity and neglect. Within the past decade, concerned citizens banded together to save this forgotten piece of Miami, rather than have it used for private development. The location has since been preserved and new recreation structures built.

There is a miniature train, an antique carousel, and a playground. The park is, obviously, a work in progress; the concession stand may or may not be open. On the park's website, there is a helpful guidebook with information about plants, birds, and sea life, which you can download for free. Historic Virginia Key Beach Park still charges guests, despite the "no swimming" policy. Park entrance is $6 per vehicle, 7 days a week. Open only on weekends, the Miniature Train Ride costs $1 and the "Allan Herschell" Vintage Carousel costs $1 a ride. The Bath House provides restroom facilities. There are picnic tables and grills. Unfortunately, for the moment, unless you have an aversion to the sea, it's better to save your money.

~~~~~~

Historic Virginia Key Beach Park
4020 Virginia Beach Dr.
Miami 33149
305.960.4600
http://www.virginiakeybeachpark.net
7:00 a.m. to sunset, 7 days a week except Thanksgiving and
Christmas
Ages: BT, M (if you don't mind staying out of the ocean)

~~~~~~

The crown jewels of Key Biscayne are the large, open beaches of Crandon Beach Park and Bill Baggs Cape Florida State Park. To reach Crandon Park, drive approximately 5 miles from the key's toll plaza and look for the 2 entrances on the left (the island's northeast side). Crandon's beaches are "lagoon style" and usually protected from rough waves by its sandbar. Its low, gentle waves make Crandon Beach Park one of the best options in Miami for infants and toddlers. The beaches are wide, with plenty of room for families to spread out. Lifeguards in neat, cottage-style stations watch over swimmers. Restrooms are located at convenient intervals, along with showers for washing off sand. There are also concession stands with basic snacks. Many families like to bring picnics. There are large parking lots so it's uncommon not to be able to find a space. (The exception to this rule are major American holidays, such as Memorial Day, Fourth of July, Labor Day, etc.) Crandon Beach is an easy, laid-back place to swim, lounge, eat, and play.

Many people, even locals, don't realize there is more to the park. Crandon Park Beach and Family Amusement Center offers a restored historic carousel, an outdoor roller skating rink, a dolphin-shaped splash fountain, and a beachfront playground. Old-fashioned roller skates are available for rent. Unlike the beach, the Family Amusement Center is open on weekends only, from 10:30 a.m. to 5:00 p.m. Three carousel rides cost $2. The center is also accessible to wheelchairs.

In addition to the amusement center, you can enjoy the 200-acre Crandon Gardens, with tropical foliage and lakes. The gardens once were the site of the Miami Zoo; man-made pools and walkways now remain, although the animals were moved. You can still see free-roaming Sandhill cranes, Hawaiian geese, and peacocks. To get parking for the Family Amusement Center, enter Crandon's South Beach parking lot and then park on the right side. If in doubt, ask the employee collecting entrance fees before you pay. Nearby is the Crandon Park Golf Course, a well-known stop on the Senior PGA Tour. Tee times can be booked online (http://www.crandongolfclub.com).

Crandon Beach Park
6747 Crandon Blvd.
Key Biscayne 33149

305.361.5421
http://www.miamidade.gov/parks/parks/crandon_beach.asp
$5 per vehicle weekdays, $6 weekends and holidays
Cabana rentals including cold-water shower $39 per day
Beach open sunrise to sunset; office hours 9:00 a.m. to 5:00 p.m., 7
 days a week
Ages: B/T, M, TW, TN

 NECESSITIES

To buy sunscreen, beach supplies, diapers, and snacks, you will
need to drive past the park entrances into the Village of Key
Biscayne. The CVS drug store and pharmacy is at 726 Crandon
Boulevard (305.365.4621). In summer, the store should sell beach
umbrellas, which you may want for some protection from the sun.
(A garden trowel or sand shovel makes securing the pole into the
sand easier.) For cold drinks and snacks, there is also the 7-11 convenience store at 51 Harbor Drive.

To reach the other major beach attraction, Bill Baggs Cape
Florida Park, you will drive to the very end of Crandon Boulevard. On the way, you will go through the center of the Village
of Key Biscayne. This can be a good place to stop for lunch or
pick up supplies for a picnic. (See Restaurants section below for
suggestions.)

The Village is also where your family can rent bicycles to tour
the island on Key Biscayne's bike paths. Mangrove Cycles rents
bikes for adults, youth, and smaller children, along with add-ons
such as a child's seat, child trailer, and tag-a-long. Helmets are
available. Their website lists rates and other helpful information.
The Safety section of the "Practicalities" chapter suggests using
great caution when cycling, because some Miami drivers don't
seem even remotely familiar with basic traffic laws. This is true,
even on well-policed Key Biscayne. Ask shop staff for the safest
routes, and keep an eye out for cars.

Mangrove Cycles
260 Crandon Blvd., #6
Key Biscayne 33149
305.361.5555
http://www.mangrovecycles.com
Ages: B/T, M, TW, TN

At the end of Crandon Boulevard, you will find the entrance to Bill Baggs Cape Florida State Park, with a ranger booth to collect tolls and distribute maps. As a state park, Bill Baggs has been thoughtfully nurtured, with trees, beach grasses, and mangrove wetlands showing visitors how south Florida appeared before modern development. In 2013 "Dr. Beach" ranked Bill Baggs as one of the top 10 beaches in America. The beaches here are beautiful, with clean sand and terrific views. Large restrooms and multiple showers are located near the parking lots. There are rentals available: bicycles, including tandems, 4-person carts, beach umbrellas, beach chairs, kayaks, and hydrobikes.

No lifeguards oversee the beach at Bill Baggs. The waves here, while modest, are *occasionally* larger than at Crandon Park. More of a concern is the distinct and even strong current that runs parallel to shore. Watch to ensure that your child isn't tugged away from you by the current. Although plenty of people bring babies and toddlers, for truly gentle paddling Crandon or Hobie beaches are a surer bet.

One of the most popular activities is a guided tour of the historic Cape Florida Lighthouse and lightkeeper's cottage. These are led twice a day, at 10:00 a.m. and 1:00 p.m. every day except Tuesdays and Wednesdays. Children need to be 8 or older to climb the lighthouse stairs. You can also climb the lighthouse without a tour. This activity is not recommended for anyone in the family who suffers from fear of heights, claustrophobia, or asthma attacks brought on by physical exertion.

If you bring your fishing tackle, you'll find good fishing along the seawall from designated fishing piers. From the seawall you can often spot small houses that seem to hover over the water

A view of Bill Baggs beach from the Cape Florida Light.
Photo by Zickie Allgrove.

in the distance. This is Stiltsville, a collection of wood-frame homes on wood or concrete piles. "Crawfish Eddie" Walker built the first recorded house here in 1933 to avoid the city's gambling laws. For decades the remote houses provided their lucky owners with a stunning place to relax and enjoy themselves. The National Park Service wanted to demolish them, but after a public outcry, an accommodation was made and the Stiltsville Trust established.

Bill Baggs Park has various hiking trails, which go inland and in places border the water and mangroves. Routes can be difficult to tell apart on the park map, and truth be told, the trails are restful but can be a little monotonous for children hoping for spectacular wildlife sightings. Birders with binoculars have better luck. Boaters can anchor overnight in No Name Harbor for a fee; restrooms, a rinse shower, and pump out are available. Bill Baggs Park has 2 casual restaurants, which are listed in the Restaurants section below.

Bill Baggs Cape Florida State Park
1200 Crandon Blvd.
Key Biscayne 33149
301.361.8779
http://www.floridastateparks.org/capeflorida
$8 per vehicle, $2 per pedestrian
8:00 a.m. to sunset, 365 days a year
Ages: B/T, M, TW, TN

Restaurants

AYESHA INDIAN RESTAURANT

328 Crandon Blvd., Key Biscayne 33149, 786.953.4761, http://www. ayeshasaffron.com

Ayesha is a family-friendly spot. Whether you adore Indian food or want to try it for the first time, you'll find crowd pleasers such as chicken tikka masala and vegetable samosas. Reservations accepted. Closed Mondays.

BOATER'S GRILL

Bill Baggs State Park, 1200 Crandon Blvd., No Name Harbor, Key Biscayne 33149, 305.361.0080, http://www.lighthouserestaurants.com

Despite its unbeatable harbor view and laid-back Florida vibe, even many Miami residents have never discovered Boater's Grill, which is located inside the state park. After paying your entrance fee look for the access road and take a right. Cuban food and seafood are served upstairs on a covered, open-air veranda. The simply prepared pan-seared whole fish with a choice of sides (including delicious Cuban fried plantains) is the standout. Whole fried fish starts at $28.95; other fish dishes and kids' meals are much less expensive.

DONUT GALLERY DINER

83 Harbor Dr., Key Biscayne 33149, 305.361.9985, http://www.donutgallerydiner.com

The tiny Donut Gallery cooks up tasty, inexpensive diner food like pancakes and BLT sandwiches but does not serve donuts (or doughnuts)! Opened in 1972, this Key Biscayne landmark has black vinyl stools, laminate counters, and good prices.

FORNO E FORNELLI

328 Crandon Blvd. #111, Key Biscayne 33149, 305.365.5240, http://www.fornoefornelli.com

Fresh ingredients contribute to delicious coal-oven pizzas and yummy pastas such as penne *arrabiata* and lasagna. Dinner pastas run about $15 to $18, while pizzas that can be shared start at $14. Reservations accepted.

LA BOULANGERIE

328 Crandon Blvd., Key Biscayne 33149, 305.365.5260

This small restaurant sometimes gets crowded for breakfast and lunch; fresh croissants and baguettes can be eaten there or taken out. Eggs, pancakes, and pastries are served in the morning, with sandwiches and pastas for lunch.

LIGHTHOUSE CAFE

> Bill Baggs State Park, 1200 Crandon Blvd., Key Biscayne 33149,
> 305.361.8487, http://www.lighthouserestaurants.com

The Lighthouse Cafe has a bargain breakfast menu, featuring omelets, pancakes, and French toast. For lunch, hot dogs cost a mere $2, while a salmon burger is a modest $7.95. More elaborate meals such as paella, pasta, and fish dishes are also on offer. Both breakfast and lunch menus are available on their website. This open-air restaurant is situated a short walk from the ocean and is very family-friendly. Open 9:00 a.m. to sundown every day.

OASIS CAFE

> 19 Harbor Dr. (at Crandon Blvd.), Key Biscayne 33149, 305.361.9009

Here you'll find inexpensive Cuban food with open-air seating in a very casual setting. Try the roast pork Cuban sandwich or a thin *palomilla* steak. You can also order food to go. Cuban black beans and white rice are a favorite for many Miami kids, along with fried plantains.

OLD HEIDELBERG DELI

> 328 Crandon Blvd., Key Biscayne 33149, 954.463.3880

This German deli makes delicious sandwiches, sausages, salads, breads, and hot dishes. It makes for a good quick stop when putting together a beach picnic.

Accommodations

Key Biscayne does not have many hotel options. In general it can be expensive to overnight in the Village. Besides the 2 options listed below, you can additionally find condo rentals on Vacation Rentals By Owner (http://www.VRBO.com) and http://www.home away.com.

💰 SPLURGE

RITZ-CARLTON KEY BISCAYNE

455 Grand Bay Dr., Key Biscayne 33149, 305.365.4500, http://www.ritzcarlton.com/en/Properties/KeyBiscayne

This luxurious hotel has 2 heated swimming pools, 11 tennis courts, 4 restaurants, and a 20,000-square-foot spa and salon. The Ritz Kids activity program is designed for ages 5 to 12; there are spa treatments designed for 'tweens and teenagers. The hotel has a longer-than-average children's menu; you can opt for a child's breakfast-lunch-dinner option at $35 per day. Low season rates start at $299, while the Presidential Suite can set you back more than $2,000. Expect the comforts of this world famous chain, along with a pleasant if somewhat narrow beach, expensive valet parking, and pricey drinks.

SILVER SANDS BEACH RESORT

301 Ocean Dr., Key Biscayne 33149, 305.361.5441, http://www.silversandsbeachresort.net

Simple motel rooms, oceanfront units, and cottages come with kitchenettes and are decorated in a style that is retro (some reviewers say "out-of-date") and basic. A heated pool, playground, free parking, and beachfront location define Silver Sands' amenities. No extra charge for children under 16 (limited to 2) when sharing a room with parents. Off-season daily rates start at $129; weekly rates start at $839. It is worth reading reviews on websites such as TripAdvisor to see if this property matches your family's expectations.

Coconut Grove

If you poke around the back streets of Coconut Grove, you'll come across canopies of oaks, thick tangles of palms, and gumbo limbo trees. Bougainvillea vines flowering with vibrant fuchsia petals climb over fences that may conceal wooden cottages or modern mansions. If you're fortunate, you'll spy a roving band of wild peacocks with shimmering blue tails or hear the squawk of small green parrots flying overhead. In Coconut Grove's heart lies a small downtown with walkable restaurants, shops, and hotels. Although "the Grove" itself has waterfront but no beach, Key Biscayne is only minutes away, and South Beach (outside of rush hour) is a 15- to 20-minute drive. The sights of Coral Gables, Little Havana, and Downtown are all within convenient driving distance, and in the case of Downtown, reachable by Metrorail.

Coconut Grove began life as one of Miami's original neighborhoods. Settlers carved homesteads out of tropical hammock and braved hurricanes and thick swarms of mosquitos to create a paradise on the shores of Biscayne Bay. After the Third Seminole War ended in 1858, American pioneers traded with the Indians. Black Bahamians, who came in the late 1800s to work in hotels, established a neighborhood called Kebo (today known as Village West). If you want to show your family what life was like when pioneers lived in wood-frame homes on a remote coast, your best bet lies within a Florida state park in Coconut Grove.

That is not to say that nothing has changed: determined "Grovites" have been fighting the steamrollers of modernity since the 1920s, often without success. Coconut Grove has its shopping developments and tall hotels (some with incredible marina views). Nevertheless, the hopping pace of Miami changes once you cross into the Grove. The rhythm slows a little, people become somewhat more courteous, and if you know where to look, you can still catch a glimpse of another era.

During the 1960s and 1970s, folk singers, rockers, and hippies turned Coconut Grove into a major hangout and protest spot. The Grove's counterculture, groovy atmosphere has all but disappeared, leaving an offbeat spirit most visible during yearly events such as the Coconut Grove Arts Festival (February), the Coconut Grove Bed Race (September), the Mad Hatter Arts Festival (November), and the cheeky King Mango Strut parade (before New Year's). A fantastic blog, http://www.coconutgrovegrapevine. blogspot.com, announces dates and times for upcoming street fairs, parades, and happenings and reports on local Grove issues.

One of the most underrated but memorable sites to explore in Miami is the Barnacle Historic State Park. In 1886 shipbuilder Ralph Middleton Munroe abandoned chilly Staten Island, New York, to make his permanent home in a barely inhabited swath of land on the bay. Munroe first heard of this place from settler William Brickell and visited with his wife, Eva, in hopes that the warm weather would help her recuperate from tuberculosis. (It did not. Eva died, devastating Munroe. He later married Jessie Wirth.) "Green" before the term even existed, Munroe drew inspiration from the philosophy of family friends Ralph Waldo Emerson and Henry Thoreau. He constructed a boathouse and then a house in 1891 that stood in harmony with the surrounding nature. The Barnacle was originally just 1 story, but after his family grew, Munroe raised the original structure on pilings and added another story underneath. He, Jessie, and their children

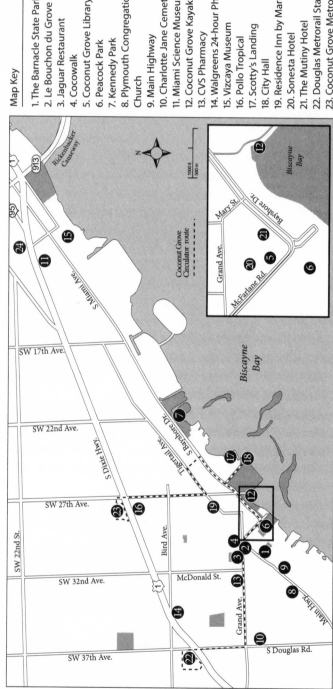

Coconut Grove

Map Key

1. The Barnacle State Park
2. Le Bouchon du Grove
3. Jaguar Restaurant
4. Cocowalk
5. Coconut Grove Library
6. Peacock Park
7. Kennedy Park
8. Plymouth Congregational Church
9. Main Highway
10. Charlotte Jane Cemetery
11. Miami Science Museum
12. Coconut Grove Kayak & SUP
13. CVS Pharmacy
14. Walgreens 24-hour Pharmacy
15. Vizcaya Museum
16. Pollo Tropical
17. Scotty's Landing
18. City Hall
19. Residence Inn by Marriott
20. Sonesta Hotel
21. The Mutiny Hotel
22. Douglas Metrorail Station
23. Coconut Grove Metrorail Station
24. Vizcaya Metrorail Station

A child's bedroom with dolls and a baby carriage at the Barnacle.
Photo by Zickie Allgrove.

Patty and Wirth were pioneers of early Coconut Grove and Miami. Munroe became a well-known boat designer, commodore of the local yacht club, and a photographer. He also combatted typically shortsighted schemes such as using Biscayne Bay as a dump for the area's raw sewage.

Munroe's descendants sold his bay-front property to the State of Florida for a bargain price so that future generations could see untouched tropical hammock and appreciate the late-19th century home. The Barnacle's windows were designed to catch ocean breezes and the kitchen pump installed to bring freshwater into the house. The children's bedrooms with their handmade toys will be especially interesting for little ones. The 30-minute guided tour of the house can be made even more child-friendly by asking your kids in advance: Where did people use the bathroom? How did they "air condition" their house? What appliance in the kitchen cost as much as a new car?

The boathouse and a replica of Munroe's 28-foot boat *Egret* add to the overall authenticity. Parking is available on the street and in a lot beside the shuttered Coconut Grove Playhouse (3500 Main Highway). Check the Barnacle Society's website (http://www.thebarnacle.org) for special events; there are "Barnacle Under Moonlight" concerts on the grounds, with paid admission, when visitors can bring picnic dinners (or takeout meals from nearby restaurants). The sense that you're sitting within a landscape much as it was 100 years before, under the stars, while your children run around or dance to the tunes, can be a magical thing.

The Barnacle Historic State Park
3485 Main Highway
Miami 33133
305.442.6866
http://www.floridastateparks/thebarnacle
Park entrance $2 per person
Tours: Adults $3, children $1 (6–12), children under 6 free
Friday through Monday 9:00 a.m. to 5:00 p.m.
Guided tours Friday through Monday, 10:30 a.m., 11:00 a.m., 1:00 p.m., 2:30 p.m.
Closed Tuesdays, Thanksgiving, Christmas, and New Year's
Ages: M, TW, TN

Once you leave the Barnacle, you are literally within Coconut Grove's miniature "downtown," where you can eat lunch or dinner, savor a frozen yogurt, and browse local shops. The Olfactory Company sells European soaps, candies, and toys (3444 Main Highway), while steps away Brenda's Boutique sparkles with little girl headbands, hair ribbons, dresses, and jewelry (3444 Main Highway). Design Box contains an appealing selection of home accessories, jewelry, and art (3197 Commodore Plaza); a few doors down at 3155 Commodore Plaza, the This and That Shop, a church-operated thrift store, occasionally yields treasures such as a Lilly Pulitzer dress or a nifty pair of palm tree sconces. Hidden inside a convenience store at 3135 Grand Ave is Asian Thai Kitchen, which prepares Crispy Duck Curry, Shrimp

Coconut Grove's small downtown, at the intersection of Main Highway, Grand Avenue, and McFarlane Road. Photo by Zickie Allgrove.

Pad Thai, and other authentic Thai cuisine for delivery or takeout (305.323.9294). Shopping and dining are concentrated within streets Main Highway, Commodore Plaza (named after Commodore Ralph Munroe), and Fuller Street, as well as a stretch of Grand Avenue. International cuisine abounds, from Peruvian to French to Indian; see the Restaurants section below for suggestions.

⊘ SURVIVAL TIP

Information booths brightly painted with tropical flowers by local artist Eileen Seitz are situated on Main Highway near the Barnacle, on Grand Avenue in front of the post office, and in front of Cocowalk. The booth at Cocowalk is the one most frequently manned and provides information on local events and directions.

♀ INSIDE SCOOP

The Kirk Munroe Tennis Center at 3101 Florida Avenue is named after a famous writer and conservationist who penned boys' adventure tales. Together with his wife, Mary Barr, Kirk Munroe (no relation to Ralph) helped found Coconut Grove in the late 1800s. He also built the first tennis court in Miami. Located 1 block north of Grand Avenue, off Matilda Street, the center's 5 courts have recently been resurfaced. A daytime court costs $3 per person for noncity residents and 50¢ per child. There are restrooms, water fountains, and a shaded playground, too.

🚼 NECESSITIES

At 3215 Grand Avenue, just west of McDonald Street (a.k.a. 32nd Avenue), the CVS drugstore is a convenient place to buy diapers, sunscreen, cold drinks, and pain relievers. It's open until 10:00 p.m., but the pharmacy closes at 9:00 p.m. (305.569.1161). A 24-hour Walgreens is located at 3490 Bird Avenue (305.446.5037). Milam's at 2969 McDonald Street (32nd Avenue) and U.S. 1 sells groceries and delicious fresh produce.

If you walk a bit further from the Barnacle, to the intersection of Main Highway, McFarlane Road, and Grand Avenue, you'll spot Cocowalk, a 3-story shopping development with local and chain businesses (including Crocs, Victoria's Secret, Gap and Gap Kids, Chili's, the Cheesecake Factory, and Starbucks). Romeo and Juliet serves Italian gelato and Palm Produce Resort Wear sells beach cover-ups for grown-ups. Cocowalk houses a movie theater, Paragon Grove 13, and a parking garage, making this a good option in case of rain. Teenagers may like Maui Nix, a surf shop with cool clothes and flip-flops. Cocowalk features live music on weekends and some weekday evenings in its open-air courtyard; check the website for times and bands.

A double-decker bus takes tourists by Cocowalk on Grand Avenue. Photo by Zickie Allgrove.

Cocowalk
3015 Grand Ave.
Miami 33133
305.444.0777
http://www.cocowalk.net

If you continue past Cocowalk, walking east on Grand Avenue past Virginia Street, you'll see signs pointing down a passageway for the Bookstore in the Grove (3390 Mary Street). This neighborhood shop contains a children's and young adult section, toys, guidebooks, fiction, and a café that serves coffee, desserts, and astonishingly good croissants (http://www.thebookstoreinthegrove.com). Or, leaving Cocowalk, you may want to cross Grand Avenue and follow McFarlane Road down toward the water. McFarlane Road is named for settler Flora McFarlane, who braved Miami's climate and wilderness as a single woman. On the right you'll pass the Sonesta Hotel, then the Coconut Grove Library, built on land donated by pioneer Ralph Middleton Munroe (founder of The Barnacle). Munroe's first wife, Eva, died young of tuberculosis; her grave lies in a small fenced-off area to the left of the library and is the oldest marked grave in Miami. Immediately past the library down a driveway is a coral rock clubhouse. This was once called the Housekeeper's Club, which was founded by Flora McFarlane in 1891. The club brought a sense of community and companionship to the women of Coconut Grove, who lived in relative isolation with very few comforts. (The present coral rock building was erected in 1926.) Member Mary Barr Munroe included young girls by founding a subgroup for them, the Pine Needles Club, and helped them start a local library.

Across the street you'll see the wide-open expanse of Peacock Park, where innkeepers Charles and Isabella Peacock built Miami's first hotel in 1883. Peacock Park hosts several Grove events and includes a small playground and walkway beside the mangroves to view the water. Occasionally, homeless gentlemen and old sailors congregate under the oaks for afternoon chat sessions, but they keep to themselves. Beside the park is St. Stephen's Episcopal Church, a Modern 1950s building with lots of stained glass. (For an even more developed, kid-friendly space with a shaded playground, walking trails, and fenced dog park, you'll need to drive to the nearby Kennedy Park at 2400 S. Bayshore Drive).

Before seeing other major attractions nearby, you may want to do a brief (5- to 10-minute) driving tour to get a feel for "the Grove." From the Barnacle, drive southwest on Main Highway. You'll soon encounter a canopy of trees and the lush foliage that Coconut Grove is known for. Turn right on Devon Road for a look at one of Miami's landmarks, the Plymouth Congregational Church. First founded in 1897, the charming church was built of coral rock in the mission style by a single Spaniard, Felix Reborn, in 1916 and 1917. Plymouth continues to be an important place of worship in the community, with Sunday services at 10:00 a.m.

Plymouth Congregational Church
3400 Devon Rd.
Miami 33133
305.444.6521
http://www.plymouthmiami.org

As you drive away from the church, Devon will dead-end at Hibiscus Street. Veer left and then take the immediate right onto Avocado Avenue. After 1 block, you'll take a left on Plaza Street, go 2 blocks to Palmetto Avenue, and then head left on Palmetto until you reach Hibiscus Street again. On this short drive you'll see a variety of Grove houses, from historic cottages to Mediterranean Revival mansions—and perhaps wild peacocks sauntering past. Take a right on Hibiscus and continue until you're back at Main Highway. A left turn takes you back toward downtown Coconut Grove. Residents will appreciate you driving slowly and keeping an eye out for children and other pedestrians, especially since this neighborhood does not have sidewalks.

To see a section of the Bahamian Grove (or Village West), which remains predominantly African-American, turn from Main Highway onto Charles Avenue. At 3242 Charles you'll see the late 19th century Stirrup House, built by Bahamian E.W.F. Stirrup, who constructed approximately 100 homes for local black families, in the process becoming a self-made millionaire. A short distance at 3298 Charles Avenue is the partially renovated, circa 1890 home of Mariah Brown, who is believed to have been the first black person to build a residence in Miami. Brown came from the Bahamas with her husband, Ernest, and worked for the nearby Peacock Inn. Back then, Charles Avenue was called Evangelist Street. Plans to finish renovation and turn the house into a museum about Bahamian settlers have been stymied by a lack of funding.

Continuing on Charles Avenue, you can turn right on Hibiscus Street to view the pretty pink Christ Episcopal Church, founded in 1901, or keep going on Charles to pass the Charlotte Jane Cemetery, created out of coral rock and named in honor of E.W.F. Stirrup's wife. (It was, incredibly, the setting for Michael Jackson's video "Thriller.") When you've reached Douglas Road (a.k.a. 37th Avenue), you can turn right, then take another right onto Grand Avenue to get you back to downtown Coconut Grove.

Village West has valiantly attempted to hang onto its historic roots, with a few wooden shotgun houses and clapboard cottages surviving. Those familiar with the architecture of Key West, New Orleans, and Bahamian islands will recognize a similar vernacular frame style in the limited number of remaining houses. The yearly Bahamian Junkanoo parade on Grand Avenue could be a tourist magnet, but organizers haven't recently divulged the parade times. Perhaps they want to keep the event small and local. The neighborhood has struggled with economic decline, shuttered storefronts, and pockets of violence from drug dealing. Local churches strive to provide positive, faith-based centers for the community. Visitors walking west on Grand Avenue past Margaret Street are often surprised by how dramatically the neighborhood changes, with deteriorated apartment buildings on both sides of the avenue. (Tourists shouldn't stroll here at night.) Other streets reveal modest houses with carefully tended yards. The few remaining wood-frame homes in Village West are one of Miami's only direct links back to its origins.

RAINY DAY

After a big helping of Coconut Grove history, it can be refreshing to switch gears and visit a child-focused attraction. The modest Miami Science Museum sits in northeast Coconut Grove, until a new museum opens Downtown in 2015. This well-worn facility mounts a wide range of exhibits such as Moving Things, Nano, Energy Tracker, and Sea Lab. Emphasized are hands-on learning and interactive experiences. The museum also houses the Miami Planetarium, which public television fans may recognize as the setting for the PBS television show *Star Gazer*. The planetarium shows films throughout the day, while the observatory is open the first Friday of the month from 8:30 to 10:00 p.m. At the Wildlife Center injured birds are rehabilitated. On the museum website shows and demonstrations are listed for each day.

Miami Science Museum
3280 S. Miami Ave.
Miami 33129
305.646.4200

http://www.miamisci.org
Adults $14.95, children (3–12) $10.95, children 2 and under free
10:00 a.m. to 6:00 p.m. (box office closes at 5:30 p.m.)
Closed Thanksgiving and Christmas Day
Ages: B/T*, M, TW
*While toddlers may not grasp the science, there are objects to touch and manipulate.

💰 SPLURGE

Coconut Grove is home to several marinas and sailing clubs. If you know your way around a boat, this could be a great opportunity to take your kids out on the water. American Watersports offers rentals of 22, 24, and 26 footers in the $315 to $405 range for a half-day, not including damage deposit. (More than one visitor has run a rental boat aground in shallow Biscayne Bay, so if you don't want the responsibility, take one of their private tours instead.) A 1-hour boat tour of Miami with guide runs $200. Arrangements and payment should be made in advance. Additional rates and services can be found on the website. Life jackets for children and adults are provided.

American Watersports
2560 S. Bayshore Dr.
Miami 33133
305.856.6559
http://www.americanwatersports.us
Ages: M, TW, TN

A more low-tech way to get out on the water is to rent paddleboards or kayaks. You will find rentals from a floating "office" at the Dinner Key Marina, located where 27th Avenue dead ends into Bayshore Drive. Look for the sign at the marina advertising kayak rentals. If you park next to Peacock Park it's about a 2- to 3-block walk. Some agility is required to climb from the dock to the boat/office, and from the boat into your kayak. There is calm paddling among the anchored sailboats and mangrove islands.

Coconut Grove Kayak and SUP
305.345.4104
http://www.miamicatamarans.com
Ages: M, TW, TN

Anyone who has become seriously intrigued by the Cuban history of Miami may want to visit the Ermita de La Caridad, the shrine to Our Lady of Charity, near Mercy Hospital in Coconut Grove. La Caridad del Cobre (Our Lady of Charity of Cobre) is Cuba's patron saint. The legend goes that hundreds of years ago 3 men found a beautiful image of the Virgin Mary floating in the Bay of Nipe after a storm and inscribed with the words "I am the Virgin of Charity." It has been reported that the present statue at this conical-shaped shrine was secreted out of communist Cuba in a diplomatic pouch, so as to escape confiscation. The Ermita has been a focus of Cuban exile life and a rallying point for Miami's Cuban community at various times of crisis. Children may be fascinated by the elaborate costume the Virgin statue wears. If you see women dressed all in white, with their hair covered, these are probably *santeras* (or novitiates) who are there to honor Oshun, the orisha of love in Santeria. Santeria is a religion with African roots, which acquired the trappings of Catholicism in Cuba in order to survive during Spanish colonialism. Followers of Santeria revere the image of the La Caridad del Cobre as a symbol of Oshun—which explains why they come to this shrine. However, La Ermita is a Catholic place of worship, and Cuban Catholics who pray at this shrine appreciate visitors entering this holy space respectfully. Sunday Mass is celebrated at 3:00 p.m. and 6:00 p.m.

Ermita de la Caridad
3609 S. Miami Ave.
Miami 33133
305.854.2404
http://www.ermitadelacaridad.org

The grand gatehouse entrance to Vizcaya, the mansion
built by James Deering. Photo by Laura Albritton.

The final destination in Coconut Grove is Vizcaya, an ornate
mansion built on the water in 1916. Unlike the Barnacle's simple
settler beauty, Vizcaya boasts opulent decoration and ornate
antiques. When Miami was still an insignificant, barely populated backwater, industrialist James Deering hired a veritable
army—thousands of workers—to erect this massive home, with
its thirty-four Renaissance and French-influenced rooms. Vizcaya remains a monument to an American entrepreneur who
fell in love with European splendor; it has hosted kings, queens,
presidents, and a pope. The museum offers a guide, "Exploring
Vizcaya with Young Visitors," that helps parents make the tour
entertaining for kids. Even so, it may be wise to pick and choose
a few rooms of the mansion to focus on. Children generally enjoy the grounds best of all, with their pretty statuary, grotto,

bridges, and gardens. Only single-sized strollers are allowed within the house. In the garden there are some uneven surfaces, gravel, and steps that may be challenging with a stroller or for a toddler. Vizcaya has a café with a children's menu.

Vizcaya Museum and Gardens
3251 S. Miami Ave.
Miami 33129
http://www.vizcayamuseum.org
Adults $18, children (6–12) $6, children 5 and under free
9:30 a.m. to 4:30 p.m.
Closed Tuesdays, Thanksgiving, and Christmas
Ages: B/T, M, TW, TN

Restaurants

These listings give you just a selection of Coconut Grove's restaurants. Not described here due to space constraints are the chains in Cocowalk (Chili's, Cheesecake Factory, Starbucks) and Johnny Rockets directly across the street on Grand and McFarlane.

BOMBAY DARBAR

3195 Commodore Plaza, Miami 33133, 305.444.7272, http://www. bombaydarbarrestaurant.com

If Indian food sounds appealing, go to Coconut Grove's Zagat-rated Bombay Darbar for delicious treats such as pakoras, creamy chicken korma, vegetarian channa masala, and lamb roganjosh. If you're trying Indian food for the first time, the tandori chicken, served with basmati rice, makes for an easy start. Closed Mondays. Reservations highly recommended for weekend nights.

LE BOUCHON DU GROVE

3430 Main Highway, Miami 33133, 305.448.6060, http://www. lebouchondugrove.com

Le Bouchon serves French comfort food in a congenial setting. The lack of children's menu isn't a problem for breakfast or lunch (with pancakes, French toast, and eggs on offer) but becomes trickier for dinner; the chef will prepare a plain chicken breast with fries for kids, or you could share a *steak frites*. The *salade du Bouchon* is *délicieux* for lunch, as is *le filet de boeuf poêlé* for dinner. Reservations recommended on weekend nights.

JAGUAR CEVICHE SPOON BAR AND LATAM GRILL

3067 Grand Ave., Miami 33133, 305.444.0216, http://www.jaguarspot. com

Jaguar serves fresh Peruvian *ceviches* along with tasty Latin American dishes and excellent cocktails. Be warned: the Celia's chopped salad is addictive. Parents can try a *michelada* beer (with a healthy quantity of lime juice in a salt-rimmed glass) or a chilly Brazilian *capirinha*. Some children may enjoy the quesadillas, a side dish of black beans and rice, or homemade fries and potato chips. If waitstaff don't mention it, be sure to ask about the small selection of kid-sized dishes not listed on the menu. On Saturday and Sunday brunch is served.

THE LAST CARROT

3133 Grand Ave., Miami 33133, 305.445.0805, http://www.lastcarrot. com

This small storefront concocts delicious smoothies, juiced vegetables, homemade soups, and sandwiches. Vegetarian options include hummus pita, tofu pita, and spinach pie.

 DEAL

POLLO TROPICAL

2710 S. Dixie Highway, Miami 33133, 305.448.9892, http://www. pollotropical.com

Pollo Tropical is Miami's favorite fast-food chain, with Caribbean and Latin American–style meals. Popular dishes include the chicken or pork TropiChop (grilled, chopped meat on a bed of black beans and rice). Pollo Tropical also has a children's menu and a range of side dishes, soups, and desserts.

♀ INSIDE SCOOP

SCOTTY'S LANDING

3381 Pan American Dr., Miami 33133, 305.854.2626, http://www. sailmiami.com/scottys

With a gorgeous view of the marina and bay, Scotty's Landing is the true Coconut Grove insider's secret. Drive onto Pan American Drive as if you're going to City Hall, then veer left into a small parking lot. Next walk through the boatyard until you spot the green and white canopy on the water. Come on Friday nights if you want to hear mellow music. Two of the best things on the menu are the cheeseburger (like in the Jimmy Buffett song) and the smoked fish

The marina at Scotty's Landing restaurant, just next to Miami's City Hall. Photo by Zickie Allgrove.

dip. There is no children's menu but plenty of items for kids including fish strips, chicken fingers, and a BLT. The City of Miami cur-
rently plans to replace Scotty's with something flashier and more
upscale. As of this writing, Scotty's remains open. Call to confirm
it's still going strong.

PANORAMA

2889 McFarlane Rd., Miami 33133, 305.447.8256, http://www.
panorama-restaurant.com

Located on the eighth floor of the Sonesta Hotel, the stylish
Panorama serves Peruvian and American food with an amazing
view of the marina. The children's menu provides kid favorites
(including a hamburger with fries). Adults might try the *ceviche*
or *tiraditos* appetizers, the steak dish *tacu tacu a lo pobre con lomo*,
or the *jalea mariscos*, a decadent fried seafood tower. For the best
view of all, come half an hour before sunset.

Accommodations

Select Coconut Grove hotels are detailed below. Additional properties not described for lack of space are: the Mayfair Hotel, the
Marriott Courtyard, the Ritz-Carlton (which does not offer the
children's amenities provided at the Ritz on Key Biscayne), and
a Hampton Inn (just off U.S. 1 and 27th Street). Apartments,
houses, and rooms can also be found on http://www.airbnb.com,
although note website and cleaning fees.

THE MUTINY

2951 S. Bayshore Dr., Miami 33133, 305.441.2100, http://www.
providentresorts.com/mutiny-hotel

Just around the corner from the Sonesta, the Mutiny can be
less expensive, with a low season 1-bedroom suite that can sleep
2 adults and 2 children going from $159 to $199 per night. A
good waterfront location, smallish pool in attractive outdoor
setting, kitchens, pay internet access, washer/dryers, an Asian

restaurant, and subdued British Colonial décor define this property. Hotel parking is expensive; self-parking is available around the corner next to the Sonesta.

RESIDENCE INN BY MARRIOTT COCONUT GROVE

2835 Tigertail Ave., Miami 33133, 305.285.9303, http://www.marriott.com

Not to be confused with the Marriott Courtyard in Coconut Grove, this hotel is geared for people who want full kitchen facilities. Rooms and public spaces may be on the dated side, but if you need ample space, a low season room with king bed and sofa bed runs $129 and a 2-bedroom suite starts at $150 a night. It is worth searching the internet for the best rate. Pool, workout room, free breakfast buffet, and free Wi-Fi.

SONESTA BAYFRONT HOTEL COCONUT GROVE

2889 McFarlane Rd., Miami 33133, 305.529.2828, http://www.sonesta.com/coconutgrove

Public spaces, gym, and pool deck are sleek, stylish, and contemporary. On the eighth floor open-air pool deck, your children can swim in the saline pool or you can relax in the spa pool, while enjoying the view of the bay and marina; grab a bite at the restaurant Panorama (with children's menu). Self-parking next door is a better deal than valet. The hotel is in walking distance to the Grove's shops and restaurants, as well as Peacock Park. A low season 1-bedroom suite sleeping 2 adults and 2 children runs approximately $265 per night. Be sure to get a marina view.

Transportation

Part of Coconut Grove is walkable, while the rest will need to be seen by public transportation, taxi, or car. Some hotels (the Sonesta and the Mutiny) are within walking distance of Cocowalk, downtown Coconut Grove, and the Barnacle. The Coconut Grove Circulator, bus 249, is a public shuttle that drives in a continuous loop from the Douglas Road Metrorail station, along Grand Avenue, over to South Bayshore Drive and City Hall and ends at the Coconut Grove Metrorail station at 27th Street. The Circulator costs 25¢ per person. From the Coconut Grove Metrorail station, you can take the Metrorail to the Vizcaya station (from which you can trek to the Vizcaya museum) or to Government Center, the station in Downtown Miami. The Metrorail costs $2 per person.

Many visitors prefer to see Miami by car. The closest car rental office is the Enterprise at 3621 S. Dixie Highway (305.648.4306), while all major rental companies are found in the Rental Car Center at the Miami Airport. Sometimes taxis can be found at the hotels, or you can call Super Yellow Cab at 305.888.7777 or 24/7 Yellow Cab at 305.244.4444.

South Beach

Connected to mainland Miami by causeways and bridges, Miami Beach is actually a series of slim barrier- and man-made islands that run parallel to the coast. Originally there wasn't much habitable land here—mostly just tangles of mangrove swamp. Back in 1870, two optimistic brothers, Charles and Henry Lum, bought 165 acres and tried to farm coconuts. Due to a minor but insurmountable hitch—wild rabbits kept devouring their seedlings—coconuts on the beach never were a commercial success. After years of failure, the Lums gave up and turned over their land to a Quaker from New Jersey named John Collins. Insects, humidity, and tropical storms did nothing to deter Collins—and still the coconut farming did not thrive. He had better luck starting in 1907 with avocados, mangos, bananas, and potatoes.

Then Collins's family had a brainstorm: growing crops wouldn't make them rich, but promoting the oceanfront might. So they founded the Miami Beach Improvement Company. What about Miami Beach needed improving? The answer is just about everything. The dream was to create a paradise, but the reality stood in stark contrast: swampland, stubborn saw palmetto, yucca, and mangroves that even muscled workers could barely budge, and of course, no roads and no bridges. No one could call the early Miamians wimps.

The year was 1913, not long before the guns of the Great War began pounding Europe, but on barrier islands off the southern Florida peninsula, the battle being fought was against the limits that nature imposed. Cars, now mass-produced, were the latest craze, but to get cars—and investors with cash—across Biscayne Bay you needed a bridge. Already John Collins had sold Lummus brothers James and John 400 acres of land to develop into houses. Collins and his son-in-law Thomas Pancoast borrowed money to build what was going to be the longest wooden bridge in the world. But before it was completed, they ran out of funds.

Why has Miami always attracted wildly ambitious, obsessive dreamers? Is it something in the salt air? Or the piercing blue summer light? The latitude? Whatever the reason, when Collins met millionaire Carl Fisher, their combined idealism combusted like a box of fire crackers. Fisher bankrolled the rest of the bridge in exchange for land. But Fisher had even grander aspirations: dredging Biscayne Bay, for one, to fill in all that pesky mangrove swamp on Miami Beach. Importing elephants to pull up the irritating indigenous scrub that even an army of grown men couldn't eradicate. Building luxury hotels. Creating the Miami Beach Railway, which ran on electricity. He even had his own island—Fisher Island—which is still so exclusive you need authorization to get on the ferry to reach it.

These early schemes set the transformation of South Beach in motion. Since then, other men and women have arrived with suitcases and dreams, cash and credit, and building plans. They turned once-remote farmland into some of the world's most desirable real estate: a famous vacation destination and a quirky neighborhood that some Miamians call home.

South Beach lies in the southernmost section of Miami Beach, stretching from approximately South Pointe Drive to Dade Boulevard (or 20th Street on its west side and approximately 23rd Street on its east). It is one of the most European neighborhoods in the United States: walkable, with chic outdoor cafes, shops,

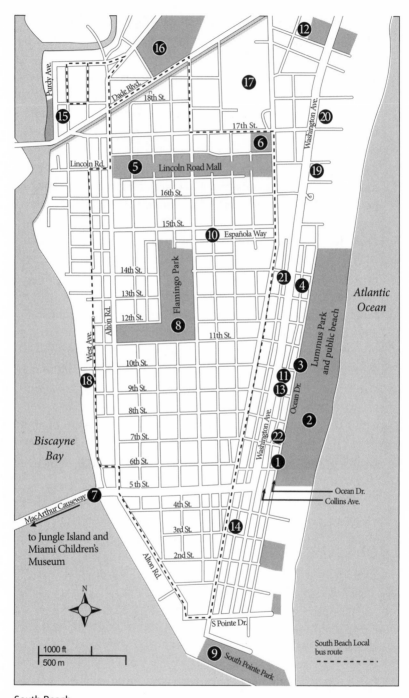

South Beach

Sunbathers lounge on rented chaises at Lummus Park beach.
Photo by Zickie Allgrove.

and restaurants, as well as beautifully preserved historic architecture. South Beach has grown famous as a nightlife capital, but it has just as much—in fact, even more—to do during the day. And if your family enjoys glamorous, urban diversity, it's an unforgettable place to visit with kids.

Some vacationers spend every day of their Miami trip on South Beach's wide, unbroken swaths of sand. The Atlantic Ocean glistens a mesmerizing aqua-blue under the afternoon sun. Funky lifeguard stations, designed to mimic the colorful Art Deco hotels across the road on Ocean Drive, dot the beach

Map Key

1. Ocean Drive	12. Bass Museum
2. Lummus Park	13. Wolfsonian-FIU Museum
3. Art Deco Welcome Center	14. Jewish Museum of Florida
4. Collins Avenue	15. South Beach Kayak
5. Lincoln Road	16. Miami Beach Golf Club
6. New World Center	17. Miami Beach Convention Center
7. MacArthur Causeway	18. Oliver's Bistro
8. Flamingo Park	19. Loews Hotel
9. South Pointe Park	20. Surfcomber Hotel
10. Española Way	21. The Clay Hotel
11. Lee-Ann Pharmacy	22. Avalon Hotel

One of the brightly painted lifeguard stations. Photo by Zickie Allgrove.

from approximately 6th Street to 14th Street. Attractive people in skimpy bathing suits parade through the surf. Despite the many gym-toned physiques, there are plenty of locals and tourists who don't look like models. The vibrant beach scene bustles with young singles, gay couples, parents with children, empty nesters, retirees, Americans, Latin Americans, Europeans, Asians, you name it. South Beach isn't for parents and kids who want a quiet, small-town beach holiday; it's for families who like to people-watch and walk to dinner. Who might go to a theme park and an art museum on the same day. It's for parents who want to spend time with their children in a lively, sophisticated environment. Summer and fall tend to be less crowded times of year, but during holidays and special events (New Year's, college spring break, the Memorial Weekend Hip Hop Festival, Fourth of July, Labor Day, and Art Basel Miami Beach) the area can grow jammed with partiers.

Whatever else visitors might come for, first and foremost they visit South Beach for the beach. So let's start there: on the sand facing the Atlantic. The ocean off South Beach usually feels temperate, ranging from a low of 71 degrees in January to a high of 86 in July. Weather and water conditions change from day to day, but often you'll see some wave action. For children who want to body surf or boogie board, it's terrific. The drop-off (how deep the water gets near shore) is fairly quick. In terms of toddlers who are just beginning to walk, sometimes the sea here can be challenging; it's not placid like Hobie Beach or Crandon Park on Key Biscayne. Dressing your baby or toddler in a flotation swimsuit is a great idea, especially on days when the ocean gets a bit rambunctious. For most teens, on the other hand, the surf just adds to the appeal of what is, without a doubt, one of the hippest beach scenes anywhere.

⊘ SURVIVAL TIP

Check out the color of the flag flying from the closest lifeguard station before letting kids dive in. Green flags mean that swimming conditions are optimal, while yellow flags encourage you to observe caution due to currents or waves. Red flags should be taken seriously: there may be rip currents or other hazards. Rip currents can pull even strong swimmers out to sea. They run along the surface, perpendicular to shore, and are often undetectable by the average person. If a lifeguard signals you to come closer in to land, or requests that your children stay out of the water, follow his or her instruction. Finally, purple flags indicate the presence of dangerous sea life, such as jellyfish. Although not known to be fatal, jellyfish stings off of Florida will feel very painful; their translucent tentacles make them difficult to see. Exercise great caution with your kids if the purple flag is hoisted.

✪✪ NECESSITIES

There are a couple of stands on the beach itself selling beverages and snacks. (Look for white kiosks.) Public restrooms can be found at the beach's entrance, near the sidewalks at 6th Street, 10th Street, 14th Street, and 21st Street. In the stretch officially known as Lummus Park, from 6th Street to 15th Street, spaced at intervals along the sand, you'll find beach chairs and umbrellas for rent. These are pricey but very convenient.

💰 SPLURGE

For truly decadent lounging, rent a beach "bed." It is hard to justify the $50 price tag, but the comfort of lounging on a raised platform with a terrycloth-covered mattress, along with the use of towels, might just seduce you. Each bed has room for 2 adults and 1 small child. You can also rent a cabana to shade the family from sun or wind.

Across from the beach, from 5th Street north to just below 15th Street runs the most happening section of Ocean Drive. Here you'll find hotels, sidewalk cafes, restaurants, bars, and shops. Ocean Drive has some of the most fascinating people-watching in the world. (If your tastes veer toward the conservative, keep in mind that outfits can be eye-poppingly scanty.) It's worth getting a table for a snack or a meal and savoring the view at least once. Outdoor dining often appeals to kids; there's a lot to look at and it feels less confining. (See the Restaurants section.) There is on-street pay parking, or parking garages at 7th Street and Collins Avenue, 13th Street and Collins, and 12th Street and Drexel.

In the 1980s far-sighted pioneers began to save and restore the neighborhood's beautiful Art Deco edifices. On the beach, from the 1920s through the 1940s, over 30 blocks of Art Deco buildings were erected. Innovative features included porthole-style windows, glass block, the use of chrome as an accent, stylized leaf and floral designs, pastel colors, neon signs, and

Bustling Ocean Drive and historic Art Deco hotels facing the beach. Photo by Zickie Allgrove.

railings that recall vintage ocean liners. Today these lovely pastel beauties are a major tourist attraction. You can see a lot just by strolling around the neighborhood. Ocean Drive is lined with historic properties: the Park Central, between 6th Street and 7th, once hosted stars such as Rita Hayworth, Clark Gable, and Carole Lombard and was designed by major Miami Beach architect Henry Hohauser, who also planned the Colony Hotel, with its fabulous neon, at 736 Ocean Drive. Art Deco master Albert Anis designed the Majestic Hotel at Ocean Drive and 7th Street. There's frequently a handsome vintage car parked in front of the fantastic Avalon Hotel at 7th Street. One block over, Collins Avenue (named for John Collins) contains several significant structures such as the 1938 Essex House (an example of maritime Art Deco designed by Hohauser) at 10th Street. Major Art Deco architect L. Murray Dixon designed the Marlin Hotel (1200 Collins Avenue), with its snazzy neon sign and bas-relief (sculptured) panels. A few blocks north at 1424 Collins Avenue is the Riviere Hotel apartment building, designed in 1935 by Albert Anis, with its stepped ziggurat parapet roofline.

If your teenagers love architecture (or if you can get your baby to nap in the stroller as you follow along), there is an entertaining Art Deco walking tour. The Art Deco Welcome Center contains a gift shop packed with creative souvenirs; they also sell self-guided tour maps. For architecture enthusiasts: pick up a copy of *Saving South Beach* by M. Barron Stofik, the riveting story of how Barbara Baer Capitman and other crusaders fought tooth-and-nail to stop the demolition of iconic Art Deco buildings.

Art Deco Welcome Center
1001 Ocean Dr. (at 10th St.)
Miami Beach 33139
305.672.2014
http://www.mdpl.org
Walking tours 7 days a week, 10:30 a.m., $20 per person

In and amongst the Art Deco buildings on Collins Avenue are several shops, most of which are geared toward adults. The Webster at 1220 Collins contains a delectable assortment of designer clothing, shoes, sunglasses, and bags, from fashion-forward labels. Spanish chain store Zara sells budget-friendly, youthful clothes at 590 Collins. Other popular stores include Kenneth Cole at 8th Street and Collins, Armani Exchange at 760 Collins, Sephora at 721 Collins, and Club Monaco at 624 Collins.

One South Beach must-see for adults and children alike is Lincoln Road, a pedestrian street with outdoor cafes, restaurants, and fantastic shopping. Designed by celebrated architect Morris Lapidus (a prime shaper of MiMo or the Miami Modern school), the street runs from Alton Road to Washington Avenue, 1 block south of 17th Street. Most South Beach locals hang out here, rather than Ocean Drive. While it's still touristy, the vibe is international, tropical cool. People-watching on Lincoln Road is never dull, with locals, tourists, jet-setters, pampered dogs, performing artists, and even an occasional movie star mingling together.

Miami parents appreciate Lincoln Road because they can linger over a meal, and no one gets in a snit if their children roam around next to the outdoor restaurant. At nine or ten o'clock at night you'll often see Latin American and local families out with their kids. Everyone's making an effort to look swell, from the mothers in their glamorous outfits to the Miami college guys in bright t-shirts and designer jeans.

The best way to experience Lincoln Road is to have dinner outdoors, then move on and get a delicious gelato as you window-shop. Or stop at a cafe for coffee drinks and hot chocolates. Parents get to enjoy a cosmopolitan, stimulating atmosphere; kids can wander a little more freely than usual, due to the relative absence of cars. At 927 Lincoln Road, Books and Books, of the beloved Miami bookstore chain, has a good children's selection, as well as a family-friendly restaurant located between Michigan and Jefferson avenues (see Restaurants section). Dylan's Candy Bar provides such a mind-boggling selection of sweet treats that kids will have a hard time choosing (801 Lincoln at Meridian Ave.). Kids may also like ArtCenter South Florida (at 800, 810, and 924 Lincoln Road between Meridian and Michigan avenues). Here you can walk through the buildings and watch artists work in their studios. All the painters and sculptors have been awarded fellowships. Entrance is free.

On Lincoln Road near Euclid Avenue is a small green area where children can run around (near Pizza Rustica). Performers sometimes appear here, including Disco Man, who will dance and give out music trivia. If you've forgotten to pack something for the little ones, there are stores such as Gap Kids, Crocs, and

The Café at Books and Books is one of the many sidewalk restaurants on Lincoln Road. Photo by Zickie Allgrove.

Alvin's Island. Lincoln Road shops for the parents include the Apple computer store, the skin care boutique Kiehl's, inexpensive Swiss watchmaker Swatch, the hip Lucky Brand jean store, bohemian clothing company Anthropologie, and the Oakley sunglass shop, to name just a few. By alternately stopping at "grown-up" stores and kid-friendly stores, everyone stays happy. At the corner of Lincoln and Alton roads, there's a multilevel movie theater, Regal South Beach Stadium 18, which usually features a children's film.

Parking can be found at 1111 Lincoln Road (at Alton Road). This Herzog and de Meuron–designed parking garage cost $65 million to build; the developer has his own penthouse on the top floor, while the high-end Alchemist boutique is found at ground level. More parking is located at 640 17th Street. Small lots offer limited places off both sides of the main strip (Lincoln Lane and Meridian, Pennsylvania, Jefferson, and Michigan avenues). If you're staying on South Beach, consider walking to Lincoln Road, taking a taxi, or taking the South Beach shuttle (see Deal below), because parking can be a pain.

One block off Lincoln Road is the New World Center, a spectacular new complex designed by American architect Frank Gehry. The center is home to the New World Symphony, an orchestral academy, and also hosts performances by internationally renowned musicians. Ticket prices to some events are quite affordable; check on their website for upcoming concerts. In addition, the center has "Wallcasts," during which live concerts are projected onto a 7,000-square-foot outdoor wall. Wallcasts are free to the public; come early for a good spot. You can bring a blanket and a picnic and listen to the music. Previous Wallcasts have featured concerts of Gershwin, Beethoven, Schumann, Tchaikovsky, and Sibelius. There is a Wallcast schedule on the website, with dates and times. The website also lists occasional, free Monday night performances and the schedule for Family Day children's concerts.

New World Center
500 17th St.
Miami Beach 33139
305.673.3331 (box office)
http://www.newworldcenter.com
Ages: B/T, M, TW, TN

 DEAL

Getting to Lincoln Road or the New World Center can be easier with the convenient shuttle bus. The South Beach Local or "SoBe Local" costs 25¢ per person and makes a loop of South Beach in two directions. It rides along West Avenue and Alton Road, all the way down to South Pointe, onto Washington Avenue, up toward the Convention Center, and then across Dade Boulevard. Make sure the bus stop has a sign for "South Beach Local" and check that the bus's digital read-out (on the front) is clearly marked as "SoBe Local." If in doubt, ask the driver.

Flamingos pose at Jungle Island, one of Miami's best attractions for children. Courtesy of Jungle Island.

In addition to its world-class beach, restaurants, and shopping, you will find 2 of Miami's best children's attractions close by: Jungle Island and the Miami Children's Museum. To get to Jungle Island, drive or take a taxi by way of the MacArthur Causeway to Watson Island. (Jungle Island also provides a free shuttle service from some South Beach and Downtown hotels. See their website for details.) Formerly Parrot Jungle in South Miami, the newest incarnation of Jungle Island contains 1.35 miles of beautifully landscaped trails, animal exhibits, and shows. The historic focus of the park was on tropical birds, and you'll still find plenty of macaws and flamingos. Today Jungle Island also hosts a wide range of exotic animals: lions, tigers, "ligers," leopards, zebus, and even warthogs. Reptiles range from snakes to an enormous albino alligator. Kids enjoy the primate exhibits with orangutans, lemurs, and baboons.

The animal shows are educational but also amusing: Winged Wonders features extraordinary birds such as the blue-necked, 6-foot cassowary and a cockatoo that rides a high-wire bicycle. The Wild Encounter show highlights the park's big cats and primates, while Dr. Wasabi's Wild Adventures will appeal to the reptile lover in your family. You may want to check out the website for daily show schedules before you visit.

Little children will especially enjoy the Petting Barn and the playground. Snacks are available throughout the park, and meals are served cafeteria-style at the Lakeside Cafe. The park has stroller and wheelchair rentals. Parking costs $8 per vehicle. If you buy your tickets online in advance, you can save $2 per person. If you plan on returning to Jungle Island within the year, the annual pass costs only $10 more per child admission and $13 more per adult.

Jungle Island
1111 Parrot Jungle Trail
Miami 33132
305.400.7000
http://www.jungleisland.com
Adults $34.95 + tax, children (3–10) $26.95 + tax, children 2 and
**   under free**
Monday through Friday 10:00 a.m. to 5:00 p.m.; Saturday and Sun-
**   day 10:00 a.m. to 6:00 p.m., 365 days a year**
Ages: B/T, M, TW

 RAINY DAY

Directly across from Jungle Island (on Watson Island) is the Miami Children's Museum, an excellent indoor option if the weather is not cooperating, or if you're simply ready for some air-conditioned entertainment. Housed in a quirky building designed by Miami architects Arquitectonica, the museum spreads over 56,000 square feet, with 14 galleries. Miami Children's Museum aspires to make learning and creating fun. The main emphasis falls on exploring aspects of the real world.

Exhibits include a pretend grocery store, a bank, a veterinarian's office, an ocean odyssey, a health center, a rock climbing wall, and more. Children have plenty of opportunity for hands-on play and movement. Children who are old enough to walk will most enjoy the activities, although the bright colors and vivid galleries may appeal to babies, too. During the summer the museum offers a children's camp, and throughout the year, they host occasional 1-day themed camps. Parking is $1 per hour.

Miami Children's Museum
980 MacArthur Causeway
Miami 33132
305.373.5437
http://www.miamichildrensmuseum.org
Admission $16, children under 1 year free
10:00 a.m. to 6:00 p.m. 7 days a week, except Thanksgiving and
    Christmas
Ages: B/T, M

⚲ INSIDE SCOOP

Another child-friendly destination on South Beach is the children's pool in Flamingo Park (next to the parking lot on 11th Street). The pool has a slide and colorful water equipment for kids to climb. Nice shallow areas are ideal for parents with babies and toddlers. Lifeguards monitor this section as well as the adult lap pool. The pool is free only to Miami Beach residents; everyone else pays admission. Technically, you pay per two-and-a-half-hour swim session; ask at the front desk if you can stay longer. (If not, be sure to pay your entrance at the start of a session. Afternoon sessions begin at 1:00 p.m. and 4:00 p.m.) Bathrooms with changing areas and showers are available, as are chairs and chaises on a first-come, first-served basis. Children 3 years and under are required to wear swim diapers. An added bonus: next door to the pool is a shaded playground with swings. Flamingo Park also has tennis courts and a fenced dog park.

Flamingo Park
1200 Meridian Ave.
Miami Beach 33139

305.673.7750
http://www.miamibeachfl.gov/parksandrecreation/
Pool admission: Adults $10, children (4–17) $6, children 3 and
   under free
Water playground, Monday through Sunday 9:00 a.m. to 7:00
   p.m., closed Tuesdays
Ages: B/T, M, TW, TN

After an active day of theme parks or swimming, a pleasant place to stroll with your kids—especially at sunset—is the recently revamped promenade at the southern tip of South Pointe. South Pointe is a South Beach neighborhood of mainly highrise condominiums south of 5th Street. The narrow park and walkway hug Government Cut, the waterway through which container ships and giant cruise ships pass; the vessels come so close it feels like you could touch them. Families, exercisers, and people out walking their dogs come to see the fantastic view. There is an interactive water feature—futuristic looking, sculpturelike spouts—that kids can play in, a playground, snack bar, restrooms, and areas for sitting. In general the City of Miami Beach produces facilities with great design, and South Pointe Park is no exception. Within the park at 1 Washington Avenue is Smith and Wollensky, the pricey steakhouse facing Government Cut. While it is not an especially child-friendly place for dinner, parents may want to get a cocktail at their outdoor cafe and patio while the children have a snack (305.673.2800). It is definitely one of Miami's best restaurant views.

After sunset if you're looking for a spot for dinner, you might try a quaint street called Española Way, which runs from Washington to Pennsylvania Avenue, north of 14th Street. Old Spanish-style buildings line this narrow road, which closes to cars at night, becoming a pleasant place to shop and dine. Al Capone once gambled at the Clay Hotel in the 1920s; in the 1930s Desi Arnaz reputedly popularized the rumba here. Española Way has served as a backdrop for *Miami Vice*, music videos, and more recently, the TV show *Burn Notice*. There is not a great deal to do, but it's a picturesque place to enjoy a meal with your children. (See Restaurants section below.)

⚐ NECESSITIES

Whether you're stocking up on sunscreen or baby wipes, you'll find several drug stores on South Beach. Lee-Ann Pharmacy is 2 blocks from Ocean Drive at 955 Washington Avenue, below 10th Street (305.531.1256). A sleek, modern Walgreens can be found at 1011 Alton Road (305.424.1145), while another Walgreens is located at 100 Lincoln Road (305.532.7909).

Even the most devoted sun-worshippers need a break from the beach sometimes. If your family wants to experience culture while not venturing far afield, South Beach has a trio of jewel-like small museums: the Bass Museum of Art, the Wolfsonian-FIU, and the Jewish Museum of Florida. The Bass Museum's permanent collection entails art from antiquity, the Renaissance, and the Baroque. Many children will enjoy the small Egyptian gallery that displays 16 objects including statuary, a sarcophagus, and a mummy. The Bass also puts on temporary exhibitions of cutting-edge contemporary art. The building itself is an attractive Art Deco structure 2 blocks from the ocean and houses a gift shop with a few items for children. (Across on 22nd Street is the Deco-inspired Miami Beach Library, which has a nice children's section.) Also, across the street there is public beach access and pay parking, making this a good location for a beach-plus-museum afternoon. Check the museum's website for upcoming Family Days.

Bass Museum of Art
2100 Collins Ave.
Miami Beach 33139
305.673.7530
http://www.bassmuseum.org
Adults $8, seniors and students $6 (with ID card), children under 6 free

Pay parking in the museum lot and perimeter streets
Wednesday through Sunday 12:00 to 5:00 p.m.
Ages: M, TW, TN

~~~~~~

You'll find the Wolfsonian-FIU museum on Washington Avenue in a restored 1927 Mediterranean Revival building. Its collections center on art and design, using objects to explore modernity and the huge social changes that have swept the world since the late 1800s. Furniture, industrial items, glass pieces, ceramics, paintings, and posters are displayed in various exhibitions. The Wolfsonian's emphasis on practical objects and advertising challenges many children's concept of a traditional art institution. After viewing the galleries your family can pause for a meal in the cute cafe or check out the design-centric gift shop.

~~~~~~

Wolfsonian-FIU
1001 Washington Ave.
Miami Beach 33139
305.531.1001
http://www.wolfsonian.org
Adults $7, seniors and children (7–12) $5, children under 6 free
Daily except Wednesday 12:00 to 6:00 p.m.; Friday 12:00 to 9:00 p.m.
Closed January 1, Memorial Day, Fourth of July, Labor Day, Thanksgiving, and Christmas
Ages: M, TW, TN

~~~~~~

The Jewish Museum of Florida is also located on Washington Avenue, in the South Pointe district. Housed in two Art Deco synagogues, the museum explores Jewish art and culture. A permanent exhibition details Jewish life in Florida, while temporary exhibitions change every few months. Of particular interest is the stained-glass window donated by notorious gangster (and temple member) Meyer Lansky, a leading crime boss who established a fortune from casinos in Las Vegas, New Orleans, and Cuba. Lansky lived on Miami Beach in the last years of his life in reduced circumstances, although many believed he'd hidden his wealth in secret accounts. Docent-led tours give an overview of the buildings and the Jewish community on Miami Beach.

Jewish Museum of Florida
301 and 311 Washington Ave.
Miami Beach 33139
305.672.5044
http://www.jewishmuseum.com
Adults $6, families $12, children over 6 $2.50, children under 6 free
Free on Saturdays
Tuesday through Sunday 10:00 a.m. to 5:00 p.m., closed Mondays, civil and Jewish holidays
Ages: M, TW, TN

For a complete change of pace, take your family to the glamorous Lucky Strike Lanes for a session of bowling. This stylish bowling alley is open to children until 9:00 p.m. (after which it has a 21 and older policy). The facility has 14 lanes, 2 pool tables, big screen TVs, a bar, and free Wi-Fi. Early afternoon may be the best time for kids, before the hopping happy hour. Adults should note that drinks can be very expensive. The pizza's pretty good.

Lucky Strike Lanes
1691 Michigan Ave.
Miami Beach 33139
305.532.0307
http://www.bowlluckystrike.com
Monday through Friday opens 11:30 a.m.; Saturday and Sunday opens 11:00 a.m.
Children welcome until 9:00 p.m.
Ages: M, TW, TN

One activity especially suited to teens is surfing. South Beach can be a fairly good place to take a surf lesson, because—unless a hurricane is imminent—the waves are often small or manageable. Children 12 to 18 years can take lessons with the South Beach Dive and Surf Center. A parent will need to sign a release for children under 18. A 90-minute one-on-one lesson costs $100; group lessons are cheaper. They also teach standup paddleboarding.

South Beach Dive and Surf Center
850 Washington Ave.
Miami Beach 33139
305.673.5900 or 305.531.6110
http://www.southbeachdivers.com
Ages: TW, TN

Many visitors don't realize that they can kayak just a few blocks from Lincoln Road. This activity is best suited for kids strong enough to wield a paddle (or you can get a double, and take them along for the ride). Families with older teens may want to reserve a spot on the Fool Moon kayak tour, which occurs at night during the full moon and includes a weenie roast on nearby Monument Island. A single kayak rents for $25 for 2 hours; a double is $40 for 2 hours. More rates are listed on their website.

South Beach Kayak
1771 Purdy Ave.
Miami Beach 33139
305.975.5087
http://www.southbeachkayak.com
Ages: M, TW, TN

Parents who like to golf with their kids will appreciate the public Miami Beach Golf Club. First opened in 1923 by Miami Beach impresario Carl Fisher, today's completely remodeled course was designed by Arthur Hill, the renowned American golf course architect. The pro shop rents both clubs and soft-spike golf shoes. (Metal spikes are not allowed.) Book tee times online or by phoning. Golf rates run $200, $125, and $100, depending on the season. Proper golf attire is required. The driving range is open 7 days a week; large buckets cost $12.

~~~~~~

Miami Beach Golf Club
2301 Alton Rd.
Miami Beach 33140
305.532.3350
http://www.miamibeachgolfclub.com

~~~~~~

Finally, no chapter about South Beach could omit one of the world's top art fairs, Art Basel Miami Beach. It only takes place once a year; hotel prices can go through the roof during this week, and the neighborhood gets very crowded. For some families, this will be an event to avoid like the proverbial plague. But if you love contemporary art, it's an incomparable experience. The main exhibition takes place in the Miami Beach Convention Center, where more than 260 galleries from around the globe show work that can fetch staggering sums. You can enroll children in Art Kids, a daycare program for parents visiting the fair run by Miami Children Museum's staff. Children 4 years and older may stay up to 3 hours in the supervised ArtKids Room; children 3 years and under may visit the room only if accompanied by a caretaker. Contact artkids@miamichildrensmuseum. org or phone 305.373.5437 extension 126 to make an advance reservation. Spaces are limited. Check the fair's website for general Art Basel ticket information and dates, which change each year.

During the event, South Beach hosts a variety of parties and off-shoot exhibitions, some of which are highly exclusive and others of which are free and accessible. Additional exhibitions on Miami Beach include: Aqua, Design Miami, Ink Miami, NADA Art Fair, Select Fair, UNTITLED, and Verge Art Miami Beach. For admission, addresses, and dates for the individual events, look on the internet, as the information changes each year. Across the water in the Wynwood District, Art Miami simultaneously exhibits a remarkable range of international art inside huge air-conditioned tents.

Miami Beach Convention Center
1900 Convention Center Dr.
Miami Beach 33139
305.673.7311
http://www.miamibeach.artbasel.com
Ages: M, TW, TN

Restaurants

South Beach has restaurants of almost every kind. While Ocean Drive fronts a gorgeous beach, the strip isn't known for its dining. That being said, it's worth having a meal there, just to be in the thick of things. Lincoln Road has many restaurants, including several Italian places that lure travelers with food displays. Española Way offers a range of international food beyond the two listed below (including Brazilian, Mexican, and Cuban). Not all restaurants offer a children's menu, but they are usually willing to make a child's dish on request. Ask before being seated. Some South Beach establishments automatically add a 15 percent tip to your bill. (Their rationale is that some European tourists assume tip is included and therefore don't tip at all.) You can always ask if a tip has been added. South Beach locals usually tip a total of 18 to 20 percent for service.

A LA FOLIE

516 Española Way, Miami Beach, 305.538.4484, http://www.alafoliecafe.com

This is a shabby-chic French cafe serving sandwiches, salads, quiche, and crepes. It's good for a quick bite or dessert, and a lot of kids love the crepes.

THE CAFÉ AT BOOKS AND BOOKS

927 Lincoln Rd. (between Jefferson and Michigan), Miami Beach 33139, 305.532.3222, http://www.booksandbooks.com

The well-known Miami bookstore runs an outdoor cafe with a good selection of appetizers, sandwiches, and main courses, along with a children's menu. Vegan items, too. The prices are reasonable, the food tasty, and the location excellent. Afterward, pop into the bookstore to browse their guidebooks, fiction, and children's books.

11TH STREET DINER

11th St. and Washington Ave., Miami Beach 33139, 305.534.6373, http://www.eleventhstreetdiner.com

This authentic Art Deco dining car is a South Beach institution. Located just 2 blocks west of Ocean Drive, it boasts a typical diner menu with some interesting additions such as an Argentinean skirt steak and a French *croque monsieur* sandwich of grilled ham and cheese. Their regular menu lists children's dishes; breakfast is served all day.

FOGO DE CHAO

836 1st St., Miami Beach 33139, 305.672.0011, http://www.fogodechao.com

At the Brazilian steakhouse Fogo de Chao, diners serve themselves salads and sides from buffets, then return to the table where they flip a card to green, indicating they're ready for gaucho chef tableside service. The choice of meats is considerable. Lunch in the elegant dining room costs $29.50, dinner $46.50; children 6 to 10 years eat for half-price. Kids 5 and under eat free. Drinks and tip are extra.

JOE'S STONE CRAB

11 Washington Ave., Miami Beach 33139, 305.673.0365, http://www.joesstonecrab.com

South Beach's most venerable dining spot, Joe's Stone Crab, has been serving crab claws, lobster, and other seafood for 100 years.

Temptations abound, from lobster tails to filet mignon. Open from mid-October to mid-May.

JOHNNY ROCKETS

728 Ocean Dr., Miami Beach 33139, 305.531.6258

While this retro-themed hamburger joint won't win any culinary awards, its burgers, hot dogs, and shakes make it the most kid-friendly restaurant on Ocean Drive.

LE CHIC FRENCH BAKERY

1043 Washington Ave., Miami Beach 33139, 305.673.5522

In the morning when you're headed to the beach, stop off here for flaky, warm croissants, *pain au chocolats*, and the amazing almond croissants. Get them to go with coffee and juices. Below 11th Street.

OLIVER'S BISTRO

959 West Ave., Miami Beach 33139, 305.535.3050, http://www.oliversmiamibeach.com

Locals love Oliver's, with its attractive tropical terrace that's beautifully lit at night. Nicely cooked fish, seafood, steaks, burgers, and pasta for lunch and dinner. It's open for breakfast, too. In the past some staff haven't been aware of the children's menu, so be sure to ask (spaghetti, chicken fingers, grilled cheese, etc.).

PIZZA RUSTICA

667 Lincoln Rd. (at Euclid Ave.), Miami Beach 33139, 305.672.2334, http://www.pizza-rustica.com

For a budget meal on Lincoln Road, locals and tourists alike flock to Pizza Rustica. The pizza is delicious, with good toppings.

PUBBELLY

1418 20th St., Miami Beach 33139, 305.532.7555, http://www.pubbelly.com

One of Miami's newest gastronomic wonders, Pubbelly serves amazing Asian-influenced gastropub fare. The menu changes seasonally; expect dishes such as duck and pumpkin dumplings and bay scallops bourguignon. This dining experience is not for every child, but rather for little foodies-in-training. At the corner you'll also find the tantalizing PB Steak and Pubbelly Sushi. Closed Mondays.

PUERTO SAGUA

700 Collins Ave., Miami Beach 33139, 305.673.1115

One block off Ocean Drive and the beach, Puerto Sagua is a loud, busy Cuban favorite, with basic interior décor. The solid, fairly priced Cuban dishes keep winning converts, from its *media noche* sandwich (pork, ham, swiss cheese, and pickles) to the *chuletas de cerdo frito* (pork chops).

SERENDIPITY 3

1102 Lincoln Rd., Miami Beach 33139, 305.403.2210

New Yorkers who know the original Serendipity's in Manhattan will want to bring their children here for desserts like the frozen hot chocolate and Strawberry Fields sundae. They also have lunch and dinner items.

SHAKE SHACK

1111 Lincoln Rd. (at Lenox Ave.), Miami Beach 33139, 305.434.7787, http://www.shakeshack.com

With its high-quality burgers, fries, hot dogs, frozen custard, and shakes, Shake Shack has been a roaring success. They also serve beer, wine, and even canine treats for lucky dogs. The $3.85 single burger won't break the bank.

TAPAS Y TINTOS

448 Española Way, Miami Beach 33139, 305.538.8272, http://www.tapasytintos.com

A pleasant place to sit outside at night, Tapas y Tintos specializes in tapas, those delicious little Spanish snacks. Kids who like *manchego* cheese, *iberico* ham, and soft European bread will be in heaven. Some nights the indoor area can grow very noisy; if you need another option consider restaurants Oh! Mexico and

Havana 1957, both at the corner of Washington Avenue and Española Way.

SARDINIA

1801 Purdy Ave. (at 18th St.), Miami Beach 33139, 305.531.2228, http://www.sardinia-ristorante.com

One of South Beach's newer locales has attracted attention for its authentic Sardinian cuisine. Dishes include veal meatballs, thin-sliced octopus *carpaccio*, *orecchiette* (little ear-shaped pastas) with wild boar sausage, and ravioli with goat cheese and spinach. Half-portions of homemade pasta can be ordered for children.

SPRIS

731 Lincoln Rd., Miami 33139, 305.673.2020, http://www.spris.cc

Spris (pronounced sprees) serves delicious thin-crusted pizzas and panini sandwiches. Tourists and locals alike have made this a Lincoln Road fixture.

YARDBIRD SOUTHERN TABLE AND BAR

1600 Lenox Ave., Miami Beach 33139, 305.538.5220, http://www.runchickenrun.com

Top Chef contestant Jeff McInnis created an award-winning location that reflects the charm of the South, while tweaking some of its dishes. Two child-friendly items are the fried chicken and homemade biscuits. The farm-to-table philosophy of Yardbird is evident at lunch, dinner, and the decadent brunch. One block east of Alton Road.

Accommodations

South Beach brims with hotels, many of them Art Deco properties that have been lovingly restored. Below is a small sample. Hotels on Ocean Drive or Collins Avenue put you right near the beach and in the midst of the action, but can be very noisy when late-night revelers return from the clubs. It can be a good idea to call the concierge before arrival and ask for a quiet room. At certain times of year (spring break, the Memorial Day weekend hip-hop festival, Art Basel, New Year's), rates at even modest properties can get stratospheric. If, on the other hand, you can manage to get away in the low or shoulder seasons, there are some relative deals. It's always a good idea to search hotel websites for multinight promotions; websites such as http://www.booking.com, http://www.hotels.com, and http://www.kayak.com often have discounted rates, too.

AVALON HOTEL

700 Ocean Dr., Miami Beach 33139, 800.933.3306, http://www.avalonhotel.com

The historic Avalon offers rooms that start at $129 for 2 adults and 2 children. The location, on Ocean Drive across the street from the beach, inserts you into the hubbub of the neighborhood. The hotel is definitely not luxurious, the free breakfast buffet is basic, and the rooms sometimes noisy, but if it's important to be smack in the middle of the beach scene, the prices here are hard to beat. The property has a fine-dining restaurant, A Fish Called Avalon, free Wi-Fi, and pool privileges at their sister hotel, the South Seas, on 17th Street.

CLAY HOTEL

1438 Washington Ave., Miami Beach 33139, 305.534.2988, http://www.clayhotel.com

The historic Clay Hotel on Española Way is one of the few budget hotels on South Beach. Their small, basic family room can sleep 4 and starts at approximately $134 a night. It's worth requesting a quiet, renovated room away from street noise. The Clay also contains a hostel, so the atmosphere is casual. Don't expect amenities. (There is no pool or restaurant.) On the other hand, it's a 2-block walk from the beach; right outside the door there are plenty of restaurants on Española Way, and it's close to Lincoln Road. Free Wi-Fi; family rooms have a small refrigerator and a microwave. The lack of an elevator means climbing stairs with luggage.

JETSET FRANKLIN

860 Collins Ave., Miami Beach 33139, 305.538.6601, http://www.
jetsetfranklin.com

If your family values independence over hotel amenities, Jetset Franklin provides futuristic "loft" apartments with all modern conveniences. Located 2 blocks from the beach in a classic Art Deco building, apartments come with kitchen, flat screen TV, and a dining area. Apartments start at $230 per night for 2 adults and 2 children. On-site management provides advice on the surrounding area. Children under 5 stay free.

LOEWS HOTEL

1601 Collins Ave., Miami Beach 33139, 305.604.1601, http://www.
loewshotel.com

The pricey, beautiful Loews is arguably the most child-friendly hotel on South Beach. Its program "Loews Loves Kids" includes the loan of children's gear and toys, children's menus, childproof kits for the room, the Pottery Barn Kids SoBe Kids Camp, plus amenities for tweens and teens such as a Gameboy and DVD lending library. The hotel and room décor are elegant and modern; its oceanfront location is unbeatable. Other amenities include a gorgeous resort-style pool area, a spa, and multiple dining options. Summer room rates for 2 adults and 2 children start at $279 (about $315 with taxes).

SURFCOMBER HOTEL

1717 Collins Ave., Miami Beach 33139, 305.532.7715, http://www.
surfcomber.com

This lovely beachfront property has beautiful rooms and a glamorous pool area. The theme is cheerful beach chic. The hotel provides cribs, play yards, child safety room kits; children receive a Kimpton Kids gift on arrival and can borrow (or purchase) animal print robes. Let the hotel know in advance if you will need any of these amenities. The concierge can also assist in arranging babysitting and rental of strollers. In "The Pasture" statues of animals will amuse little kids. Their Lantao restaurant serves

You can rent bicycles with your credit card at the DecoBike kiosks throughout South Beach. Photo by Zickie Allgrove.

Southeast Asian–inspired cuisine. Rates from $235 per night for 2 adults and 2 children (not including taxes or resort fee).

Transportation

South Beach is one of the only neighborhoods in Miami where you can get around without a car. Especially when you consider that most hotels charge $20 to $25 per night for parking here, it can cost about the same—and be less hassle—to take taxis to and from the airport, then walk and take the shuttle bus and occasional taxis to get around South Beach. An airport taxi to South Beach is about $32 plus tip. For budget travelers, the Airport Flyer (an express bus to South Beach) costs $2.35 per person and stops at the corner of Lincoln Road and Washington Avenue. Taxis are plentiful on the beach (but they won't have child seats).

That being said, of course having constant access to a car can be very convenient, particularly with children. South Beach is highly walkable, but walking here on a clear, relatively cool January afternoon is very different from going on foot in humid

August when tropical downpours can suddenly burst from the sky.

The best thing is to consider you and your children's needs, mobility, and location. If you're pushing a single child in a stroller, you don't have any limits on how far you can walk—except your own feet! On the other hand, young children who no longer use strollers may quickly tire of walking. Older kids, particularly teenagers, might like to do some touring on bicycles. There are several DecoBike stations where you can rent bicycles from an automated kiosk (http://www.decobike.com). Pay close attention to car traffic, since Miami drivers can be oblivious or reckless.

Cabs are a good option for short trips around the beach. Cabs seem most abundant on Ocean Drive, at the cross streets of Lincoln Road, and on Washington Avenue. If your family is too numerous to fit into a single cab, consider taking the South Beach Local bus for 25¢ a person (described earlier in this chapter). Usually it comes quickly, although at times you may wait for 15 or 20 minutes at the bus stop. If you plan to explore other sections of Miami, renting a car can be practical—even if it's just for a day or two. The Miami Airport has all major car rental companies, but there are a few on South Beach: Budget at 959 West Avenue (305.674.8486), Thrifty at 1520 Collins Avenue (305.604.9827), and Hertz at 1619 Alton Road (786.276.1121). Make reservations well in advance, because demand is high.

If your family wants to see more of Miami without renting a car, considering taking a Miami bus tour. Half Price Tour Tickets sells a two-and-a-half-hour tour for $25, with 2 to 4 stops. Check their website for details, online tickets, and additional tours of the Keys and the Everglades (305.444.0707, http://www. halfpricetourtickets). The bus leaves from approximately Washington Avenue and 16th Street. Big Bus Tours does a Beach Loop tour, a Miami tour, and a scenic boat cruise (1.800.336.8233, http://www.bigbustours.com). Guides point out interesting sights, and you can "hop off, hop on" in several locations.

6

Mid-Beach and Beyond

Where South Beach ends, the rest of Miami Beach—an interconnected chain of barrier islands—begins. On the Atlantic side, sandy beaches continue northward in one unbroken stretch of beige powder fringed by palm trees. Condominiums, hotels, and MiMo resorts look out onto the waves and are warmed by the rose-colored sunrise. The strip from 41st Street to 62nd Street is known as Millionaire's Row. Blocks away from the oceanfront, high-rises give way to charming homes, many with red or white tiled roofs, built in the 1920s to the 1940s. Traditional Jewish communities enjoy the ability to walk through residential streets to Shabbat services. Further on, between the North Bay of Biscayne Bay and Indian Creek, there's the velvety-green golf course of La Gorce Country Club and the exclusive surrounding villas. Further yet lies the island neighborhood of Normandy Isles, also fronting North Bay. North Beach, the historically Jewish Surfside, and the famous shopping destination Bal Harbour extend to the north and overlook the Atlantic Ocean.

Mid-Beach feels quieter than South Beach. The streets are generally not thronged with pedestrians; fewer cars cruise the

Little sandy feet at the beach.
Photo by Zickie Allgrove.

seaside roads. Even the mood seems slightly more conservative (with somewhat less skin on display). While you don't find nearly the same density of restaurants, cafes, and shops, Mid-Beach can feel like a refuge for parents who simply want the beach and nothing but the beach. Many hotels stand directly on the sand, making the walk from room to ocean a blissfully short one.

In addition to the high-rise hotels, locals and visitors have ample opportunity to access the water at public beaches. Indian Beach, for example, is located at 46th Street and Collins Avenue. This uncomplicated strip of sand on the Atlantic Ocean benefits from the same shoreline as nearby luxury hotels. You can also take advantage of the boardwalk, a raised walkway that stretches from 48th Street south to 23rd Street, with a dazzling view of the sea. The path continues (no longer raised) all the way down to 5th Street, with public restrooms along the way.

👫 NECESSITIES

Snacks, baby supplies, and sunscreen can be purchased at Walgreens, 4049 Pine Tree Drive (at 41st Street, 305.535.9737) or further north at the Walgreens at 7430 Collins Avenue (below 74th Street, 305.864.5487).

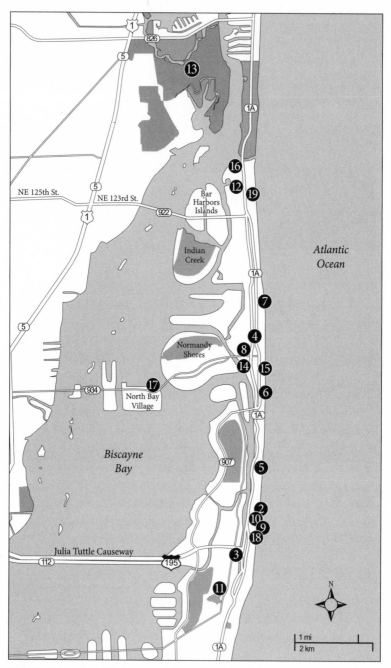

Mid-Miami Beach, Bal Harbour, and Oleta River State Park

Should Indian Beach's parking lot be full, drive north on Collins Avenue to the similar 53rd Street Beach (Collins and 53rd Street). Near the sizeable parking lot is a shaded playground with equipment for ages 5 to 12. There are public restrooms with water fountains. At approximately Collins Avenue and 65th Street is the public beach Allison Park with metered parking. Showers are provided so you can rinse off sand.

✴ DEAL

For a larger beach with more facilities, head to North Shore Open Space Park beach, which runs along Collins Avenue from 78th Street to 87th Terrace. Park across the street at the metered lots (where there are usually some free spaces). A shady area with tropical trees and shrubs gives it a natural feel. This is a mellow park, with picnic tables, grills, nature trail, bike path, showers, and restrooms; lifeguards are on duty. While beach parks on Key Biscayne charge an entrance fee, this location is free—except for the cost of the parking meter.

North Shore Open Space Park
7929 Atlantic Way
Miami Beach 33141
305.993.2032

Map Key

1. Julia Tuttle Causeway
2. Indian Beach
3. Walgreens
4. Walgreens
5. 53rd Street Beach
6. Allison Park
7. North Shore Open Space Park
8. North Shore Park Tennis Center
9. The Fontainebleau
10. Eden Roc Hotel
11. Scott Rakow Youth Center

12. Bal Harbour Shops
13. Oleta River State Park
14. Café Prima Pasta
15. El Rey del Chivito
16. Bal Harbour Quarzo Hotel
17. Best Western on the Bay Inn & Marina
18. Holiday Inn Miami Beach—Oceanfront
19. St. Regis Bal Harbour Resort

♀ INSIDE SCOOP

Miami Beach residents play tennis at the North Shore Park Tennis Center, with 12 courts and a pro shop. Nonresidents are charged $10 an hour per person. Open 8:00 a.m. to 9:00 p.m. Monday through Friday, 8:00 a.m. to 8:00 p.m. Saturday and Sunday (305.604.4080). Located at 501 72nd Street, Miami Beach 33141.

While South Beach boasts its colorful Art Deco gems, Mid-Beach showcases its own extravagant style. MiMo (or Miami Modern) is a form of architecture that reflects the optimism and energy of America after World War II. From the late 1940s to the mid-1960s, MiMo architects brought a distinctly Miami slant to modernism, with futuristic forms and flamboyant details. Mid-Beach contains 2 prized examples of MiMo architecture, whose over-the-top interiors may appeal to your kids.

The Fontainebleau at 4441 Collins Avenue remains one of Miami Beach's enduring icons. Architect Morris Lapidus conceived of an extravagant, ornate property, with glamour and bling dripping from every square inch. When the hotel opened in 1954, its combination of modernity, elaborate décor, and its location on Millionaire's Row turned it into one of the premier places to see and be seen. On the lobby floors Lapidus installed a white-and-black "bow tie" pattern, which he echoed outdoors in the swimming pool design. Lapidus himself wore a bow tie and the shape became a self-referential signature. Another famous structure is the lobby's opulent "staircase to nowhere." Celebrities from Frank Sinatra to Elvis swanked through its halls. After a $1 billion dollar renovation, the Fontainebleau's 1,504 rooms continue to attract the well-heeled and the famous. Visitors can certainly enter the lobby to take a look, or make a reservation at one of its restaurants. Those looking for a splurge may want to book a stay here and enjoy the run of this extensive property. (See Restaurants and Accommodations sections below.)

Located at 4525 Collins Avenue, the Eden Roc was a rival hotel also designed by Morris Lapidus. Opened in 1956, the building stands out as a retro wonder with its curved white façade, turquoise panels, and distinctive funnel that rises like a thick

The famous "staircase to nowhere" at the Morris Lapidus–designed Fontainebleau Hotel. Courtesy of the Fontainebleau.

smokestack on a vintage ocean liner. The Eden Roc's striking good looks and enviable location attracted celebrities such as Elizabeth Taylor, Harry Belafonte, Lucille Ball, Desi Arnaz, Ann-Margret, and Sammy Davis Jr. A renovation and a new 21-story tower have modernized the hotel but not diminished its midcentury charm. Its farm-to-table restaurant 1500 Degrees accepts reservations and is one way to enjoy the deluxe hotel if you're not staying here. (See Restaurants and Accommodations sections for more information.)

Morris Lapidus faced hostility from the architectural establishment, which regarded his work as vulgar. Strict modernists were turned off by the wild excesses of his Miami Beach buildings (not surprising considering that Lapidus's autobiography was entitled *Too Much Is Never Enough*). He once said in response to the criticism, "People want architecture to give them pleasure. They want human comfort, satisfaction, and warmth." These days MiMo has won fans the world over, and the estimation of Lapidus's contribution to architecture has grown. He not only pioneered MiMo, he also invented some of its new terms, such as "beanpoles" (slim metal poles that are decorative not structural) and "cheeseholes" (round shapes of differing sizes used to create a sense of dynamic energy).

Other Morris Lapidus–designed buildings in the Millionaire's Row section of Mid-Beach include:

Crystal House, 5055 Collins Ave. (1960)
Seacoast Suites, 5101 Collins Ave. (1963)
Seacoast Towers East, 5161 Collins Ave. (1966)

Architect Melvin Grossman, a protégé of Lapidus, designed nearby buildings:

Mimosa Condominium, 4747 Collins Ave. (1962)
The Miami Beach Resort and Spa, 4835 Collins Ave. (1962)
Imperial House Condominium, 5255 Collins Ave. (1961)

If you're curious about MiMo and want to take your children on a walking (or quick driving) tour of the Miami Modern properties on Miami Beach, one excellent resource is the website "MiMo on the Beach" (http://www.mimoonthebeach.com). Here you'll find maps and self-guided brochures about 4 different neighborhoods that you can download free. Another resource for architecture buffs is the book *MiMo: Miami Modern Revealed* by Eric P. Nash and Randall C. Robinson Jr., which contains terrific photographs and an explanation of MiMo terminology.

RAINY DAY

When the weather puts a damper on outdoor sightseeing or beach time, the Scott Rakow Youth Center contains a chilly surprise: an ice skating rink! This facility, located at the southern end of Mid-Beach, offers an excellent diversion for children. Seven days a week there are public sessions from 3:00 to 5:00 p.m. Skate rentals for nonresidents cost $4 a pair, in addition to the entrance fee.

> **Scott Rakow Youth Center**
> **2700 Sheridan Ave.**
> **Miami Beach 33140**
> **305.673.7767**
> **www.miamibeachfl.gov**
> **Adults $9, children $6**
> **Ages: M, TW, TN**

In the northern reaches of Miami Beach, Bal Harbour Village is a small, privileged community on the waterfront. Its main claim to international fame is the beautiful Bal Harbour Shops. These high-end stores are situated around a long inner courtyard, with koi pond and fountains, and tastefully landscaped

Watching orange-and-white koi at the Bal Harbour Shops.
Photo by Doug Castanedo.

with palm trees, bromeliads, and other tropical plants. Stella McCartney, Chanel, Dolce and Gabbana, Jimmy Choo, and Van Clef and Arpels are just a few of the boutiques found in the elegant shopping plaza. For adults looking to indulge, there are gorgeous designer clothes, shoes, handbags, and jewelry. Small children will delight in the enormous orange-and-white koi that swim curiously to the surface of the pond.

While no bargain hunter's paradise, Bal Harbour does contain some more accessibly priced goods among the sale racks at Neiman Marcus and Saks Fifth Avenue and at the bookstore Books and Books. For those in need of a bite, you'll find 9 options, from sandwiches to fine dining. See the Restaurants section below. Wednesdays through Sundays a complimentary shuttle takes guests to the shops from Lincoln Road, the W South Beach, the Fontainebleau, and the Eden Roc; go to http://www.balharbourflorida.com/shuttle for a complete schedule.

Bal Harbour Shops
9700 Collins Ave.
Bal Harbour 33154
305.866.0311
http://www.balharbourshops.com
Monday through Saturday 10:00 a.m. to 9:00 p.m., Sunday 12:00
noon to 6:00 p.m.

To the northwest from Bal Harbour, across the last expanse of Biscayne Bay (and not on Miami Beach) is Oleta River State Park. This calm, forested park is enjoyed by travelers and Miami residents alike, who savor getting away from city noise and embracing nature. Guests can canoe or kayak through the mangrove forest. Many people come here to use the off-road bike paths: 10 miles of intermediate trail, 3 miles of novice trail, and 4 miles of paved pathway. There is a 1,200-foot beach on the bay for swimming and lounging, although there are no lifeguards. On Saturdays and Sundays at 10:00 a.m., a park ranger leads a free nature walk that lasts an hour.

The Blue Moon Outdoor Center rents canoes, kayaks, standup paddleboards, and bikes. For sale here are beverages, food, fishing gear, bait, sunscreen, and souvenirs. They also rent beach chairs and umbrellas. Blue Moon's phone number is 305.957.3040 and their website is http://www.bluemoonoutdoor.com. The Blue Marlin Fish House, a seafood restaurant, faces the Oleta River and is open from 11:00 a.m. until 7:00 p.m. It is closed Mondays and Tuesdays. The restaurant can be difficult to find, so ask for directions when you enter the park. For those who'd rather bring their own picnic supplies, a Publix grocery store is located about 2 miles away at 14641 Biscayne Boulevard (305.354.2171).

For travelers on a budget, the rustic cabins will sleep a maximum of 4 people in 2 bunk beds or 1 double bed and 1 bunk bed. Linens and towels are not provided, so visitors will need to bring these. Some cabins have water views, and they also include an outside porch swing and picnic table. It's important to note that cabins are very simple and do not contain stoves or refrigerators. Cooking utensils and implements are not provided, and cooking must be done on ground grills. (Firewood is available at the ranger station.) Cabins contain an air-conditioning unit, but no bathroom. Restrooms with hot showers are situated a short walk away. For $55 a night or $385 a week, this is one of the best accommodation deals in Miami, for families who don't mind extremely close quarters with no TV or phone. Because cooking and eating are done outdoors, it's most enjoyable to stay in these cabins in the dry season. During the rainy season (June through October), thunderstorms and mosquitos can be an aggravation. Reservations should be made as far in advance as possible, at http://www.reserveamerica.com. Photos of the cabins can be viewed on the park's website.

Oleta River State Park
3400 N.E. 163rd St.
North Miami 33160
305.919.1846
http://www.floridastateparks.org/oletariver

$6 per vehicle
8:00 a.m. to sunset
Ages: B/T, M, TW, TN

~~~~~~

Restaurants

ARNIE AND RICHIE'S DELI

525 Arthur Godfrey Rd. (41st St.), Miami Beach 33141, 305.531.7691

A Jewish deli, Arnie and Richie's serves corned beef on rye and challah French toast to an appreciative local crowd.

CAFE PRIMA PASTA

414 71st St., Miami Beach 33141, 305.867.0106, http://www.primapasta. com

Solid, Zagat-rated Italian fare is served at this well-liked beach locale. The menu includes mussels in tomato sauce, agnolotti pasta stuffed with spinach and ricotta, and chicken parmesan. The children's dishes could be split by smaller kids. A cozy, old-school place with loads of pictures on the walls. Open for dinner.

EL REY DEL CHIVITO

6987 Collins Ave., Miami Beach 33141, 305.864.5566, http://www. elreydelchivito.com

"Chivito" means little goat, but the Uruguayan *chivitos* are actually huge, succulent steak sandwiches. Hamburgers, steaks, sausages from the *parrilla* (grill), salads, and pizza "by the yard" make up the menu at this casual spot. Open for lunch and dinner.

1500 DEGREES

4525 Collins Ave., Miami Beach 33140 (Eden Roc Hotel), 305.674.5594, http://www.1500degreesmiami.com

Chef Paula Dasilvera's farm-to-table restaurant serves skillfully prepared items such as hickory rubbed pork loin chops with polenta and dry aged Kansas City strip steak. Kids might like the side order of baked macaroni and cheese. Reservations recommended.

HAKKASAN

4441 Collins Ave., Miami Beach 33140 (Fontainebleau Hotel), 877.326.7412, http://www.fontainebleau.com

For an artistic, blowout meal that your taste buds (and your wallet) won't quickly forget, make a reservation for this trendy Chinese-fusion restaurant. Lunch on the weekdays (prix fixe $28 per person) and dim sum on the weekends are much less pricey than dinner, but no less delicious. Slow-fried sea bass with spicy black bean sauce and roasted mango duck with lemon sauce are just a couple of the tantalizing selections.

HOUSE OF DOG

456 W. 41st St., Miami Beach 33141, 305.397.8733, http://www. houseofdogmiami.com

A kosher hot dog restaurant, House of Dog serves hot dogs, burgers, and wraps with inventive toppings and craft beers. A locals' spot that is an easy outing with kids.

MANOLO

7300 Collins Ave., Miami Beach 33141, 305.868.4381, http://www. churrosmanolo.com

Crowded Manolo whips up specialties from Uruguay, including sandwiches, pizza with pancetta, and empanadas. Best of all they cook churros, those delicious strips of fried dough topped with powdered sugar.

ORIGINAL PITA HUT

530 41st St., Miami Beach 33140, 305.531.6090, http://www.pita-hut. com

Kosher falafel, shawarma, and chicken kabob sandwiches come with tahini, hummus, and Israeli salad. Other Middle Eastern dishes and children's meals are also served at this informal, busy Miami Beach spot.

SANTA FE NEWS AND ESPRESSO

9700 Collins Ave., #243, Bal Harbour 33154 (Bal Harbour Shops),
305.861.0938, http://www.santafebalharbour.com

The tuna steak, Bal Harbour burger, and smoked salmon carpaccio are tasty lunch meals offered by this casual cafe; the kid's menu contains macaroni and cheese, grilled cheese, spaghetti, hot dog, and a peanut butter sandwich.

VIDA

4441 Collins Ave., Miami Beach 33140 (Fontainebleau Hotel),
877.326.7412, http://www.fontainebleau.com

One of the least expensive ways to experience the Fontainebleau is to lunch at Vida, the resort's American-style bistro. Thin-crust pizza margaritas ($16 each) can be shared. Also on the menu are hamburgers ($18) and turkey club sandwiches ($17).

ZODIAC CAFE

Neiman Marcus, Level Three, 9700 Collins Ave., Bal Harbour 33154 (Bal
Harbour Shops), 305.993.4620, http://www.neimanmarcus.com

Zodiac Cafe is a "ladies who lunch" spot, but you don't need to be a lady to enjoy their scrumptious popovers with strawberry butter, which take the place of the usual breadbasket. Adult dishes include the shrimp Cobb salad and a seared salmon filet. The kid's menu has peanut butter and jelly, pasta, grilled cheese, and turkey roll-ups.

Accommodations

BAL HARBOUR QUARZO

290 Bal Bay Dr., Bal Harbour 33154, 305.222.7922, http://www.
quarzomiamihotel.com

This luxury boutique hotel offers an attractive, modern pool area with designer chairs and cabanas and a Zen garden. Located in pricey Bal Harbour, a room for 2 adults and 2 children, low-season, starts at $231 on internet travel sites but more typically begins at $350. Well-designed Quarzo is situated on the Intracoastal Waterway, not on the beach. Parking is $10 per night and the resort fee (which includes internet access and an evening Champagne reception) is $10 a day. Suites have kitchens. There is no restaurant on-site, but Bal Harbour eateries are nearby.

BEST WESTERN PLUS ON THE BAY INN AND MARINA

1819 79th St. Causeway, North Bay Village 33141, 305.865.7100, http://www.bestwestern.com

If you don't mind staying in North Bay Village, fronting a marina rather than the beach, this simple Best Western property could be a good budget option. Free perks include: parking, continental breakfast, Wi-Fi, and the airport shuttle. From this location, however, you'll need a rental car (or take taxis) to reach the beach and other attractions. A pool, fitness room, business center, and onsite restaurant round out the amenities. Off-season rates from $120 a night for 2 adults and 2 children.

EDEN ROC MIAMI BEACH

4525 Collins Ave., Miami Beach 33140, 305.531.0000, http://www.marriott.com

Now part of the Marriott chain, the Eden Roc showcases sleek, mod lobby spaces and crisp modern rooms. Three pools—1 adults only and 1 with a children's pool—mean guests have plenty of space to swim. The 631-room beachfront hotel contains a spa, fitness center, and dining options: 1500 Degree Restaurant, Cabana Beach Club, the Lobby Bar, and Starbucks. Rooms for 2 adults and 2 children start at $259, not including resort fee. Valet parking is $35 a day.

FONTAINEBLEAU

4441 Collins Ave., Miami Beach 33140, 305.538.2000, http://www.fontainbleau.com

This luxurious, renovated Miami Modern resort covers 5 acres and contains 9 restaurants. The enormous property boasts a top-rate spa, shops, pools, cabanas, and of course the beach. The

FB Kids program has activities planned for the afternoon (some with a fee and some free). Fridays and Saturdays the resort also has a "Kids Night Out" with children's movies so adult guests can enjoy a date night. Optimal for travelers who prize a lavish, modern aesthetic and extensive grounds. Low season rates for 2 adults and 2 children start at $359.

HOLIDAY INN MIAMI BEACH—OCEANFRONT

4333 Collins Ave., Miami Beach 33140, 305.532.3311, http://www. holidayinn.com

With low-season rates starting at $157 for 2 adults and 2 children, the oceanfront Holiday Inn is a relatively decent deal on expensive Miami Beach. A nice pool, its beach location, and pleasant lobby are somewhat offset by dated rooms. One child eats free in the Paradise Cafe with a paying adult.

💰 SPLURGE

ST. REGIS BAL HARBOUR RESORT

9703 Collins Ave., Bal Harbour 33154, 305.993.3300, http://www. stregisbalharbour.com

Located on the beach and across the street from the Bal Harbour Shops, this new St. Regis Resort is already winning great reviews. The interior design here is modern, paying tribute to MiMo architect Morris Lapidus but keeping it 21st century. The resort offers 4 dining options, a 14,000-square-foot spa, 2 infinity pools, and cabanas and daybeds on the sand. The athletic club contains first-rate equipment. The St. Regis Children's Club offers stimulating activities for children aged 4 to 12. During the week, there are the half-day camp ($55 per child) and full-day camp ($80 per child); the night camp ($65) is available on Friday and Saturday evenings and includes dinner. A 650 square foot room for 2 adults and 2 children in the summer starts at $539, not including taxes and fees.

Virginia Key's Hobie Island Beach Park with a view of the William Powell Bridge. Photo by Zickie Allgrove.

Swimming at the Virginia Key Beach and Picnic Area. Photo by Zickie Allgrove.

The Golden Dome Sea Lion Show at Miami Seaquarium. Photo by Zickie Allgrove.

A dolphin does a perfect flip at Seaquarium's Top Deck Dolphin Show. Photo by Zickie Allgrove.

Left: The historic Cape Florida Light in Bill Baggs Cape Florida State Park on Key Biscayne. Photo by Zickie Allgrove.

Below: A nature trail at Bill Baggs State Park. Photo by Zickie Allgrove.

Sailboats moored off the Coconut Grove Sailing Club and, to the right, Peacock Park. Photo by Zickie Allgrove.

The Plymouth Congregational Church in Coconut Grove. It was built by a single Spaniard in little over a year, from 1916 to 1917. Photo by Laura Albritton.

Left: Looking from the bay toward the Barnacle, the house that Ralph Munroe built in Coconut Grove. Photo by Laura Albritton.

Below: A funky lifeguard station on South Beach. The flags report current ocean conditions. Photo by Zickie Allgrove.

Right: There's often some wave action in the Atlantic Ocean off South Beach. Photo by Zickie Allgrove.

Below: Restored Art Deco hotels on Ocean Drive. Photo by Zickie Allgrove.

Left: An aerial view of Jungle Island's theater, a short drive over the causeway from South Beach. Courtesy of Jungle Island.

Below: Posing with friendly macaws at Jungle Island. Courtesy of Jungle Island.

People-watching at a cafe on Ocean Drive in South Beach. Photo by Zickie Allgrove.

A view of the MiMo resort the Fontainebleau, designed by architect Morris Lapidus. Courtesy of the Fontainebleau.

The Bal Harbour Shops draw visitors from around the world. Photo by Doug Castanedo.

The Venetian Pool in Coral Gables was created from a coral rock quarry. Photo by Zickie Allgrove.

University of Miami's Lowe Art Museum exhibits art from Asia, Africa, Europe, and the Americas. Courtesy of the Lowe Art Museum, University of Miami.

One of the striking vistas at Fairchild Tropical Botanic Garden. Photo by Zickie Allgrove.

Right: Smaller-sized equipment allows children to learn to windsurf in Matheson Hammock Park. Courtesy of Adventure Sports Miami.

Below: The Miami Marlins' fishy mascot. Photo by Zickie Allgrove.

The Deering Estate at Cutler. Courtesy of the Deering Estate at Cutler. Photo by Brian F. Call.

Above: The playground at Zoo Miami. Courtesy of Zoo Miami.

Right: Elephants at Zoo Miami. Courtesy of Zoo Miami.

Below: The Falls shopping center in the southern Miami suburbs. Photo by Zickie Allgrove.

Office buildings in Downtown. Photo by Zickie Allgrove.

Bayside Marketplace in Downtown contains shops, restaurants, and a marina. Photo by Zickie Allgrove.

Wynwood art galleries and a vibrant mural. Photo by Laura Albritton.

A street corner in the Design District. Photo by Zickie Allgrove.

Designing the foundation of a sand castle. Photo by Zickie Allgrove.

Left: A Great Blue Heron in the Everglades. Courtesy of the U.S. National Park Service. Photo by Rodney Cammauf.

Below: Mangroves are a vital Everglades habitat for fish and wildlife. Courtesy of the U.S. National Park Service.

Right: The Visitor's Center at John Pennekamp State Park in Key Largo. Photo by Zickie Allgrove.

Below: Two Key West classics, the Conch Train and Sloppy Joe's Bar. Courtesy of Florida Keys News Bureau. Photo by Bob Krist.

A sunset off Key Largo. Photo by Zickie Allgrove.

7

Coral Gables and Little Havana

From the canals that provide the well-heeled with water views to the splendid Royal Poinciana trees bursting with orange-red blossoms, Coral Gables takes its "City Beautiful" designation seriously. The city regulates which colors you can paint your house and even what kind of vehicle you can park in your driveway. (Until late 2012, pickup trucks could not be parked in Coral Gables driveways overnight. It took a court battle and finally a referendum to repeal that 52-year-old law.)

It is famous for Mediterranean-style stucco homes with red-tiled roofs and manicured yards, on streets with names like Alhambra and Granada. All of this is due to the vision of George Merrick, who dreamed of building an elegant town in the middle of rough, mosquito-ridden Florida scrub.

"Coral Gables" was originally the name of a coral rock house where the teenaged George Merrick lived in the early 1900s. As you drive past Coral Gables' graceful mansions and patinaed monuments, with their Spanish architectural references to Seville and Malaga, it may be hard to imagine that there was very little here before 1922. Merrick had been bitten by the bug of the

Coral Gables City Hall with a statue of George Merrick, the city's founder.
Photo by Zickie Allgrove.

City Beautiful movement, which aspired to fill North American cities with beauty and grandeur. With their love of fountains, plazas, green parks, monuments, and canopied streets, City Beautiful planners wanted to create a kind of civic utopia. Merrick, who inherited 3,000 acres in Miami from his father, had a free hand to apply the philosophy. As you pass streets with their distinctive (but hard to read) white road markers, it's almost surreal how carefully Merrick's original vision has been sustained.

Today, Coral Gables is one of Miami's most distinguished neighborhoods—a city within a city—and a base for the middle class, upper-middle class, and the fantastically wealthy. "The Gables," as residents call it, is known for its shopping and its

Map Key

1. Venetian Pool
2. Miracle Mile
3. Lowe Art Museum
4. The Village of Merrick Park
5. Ponce de Leon Blvd.
6. Fairchild Tropical Botanic Garden
7. Matheson Hammock Park and Beach
8. Calle Ocho (SW 8th St.)
9. Versailles
10. Marlins Park
11. Biltmore Hotel & Resort
12. Havana Harry's
13. Westin Colonnade Coral Gables

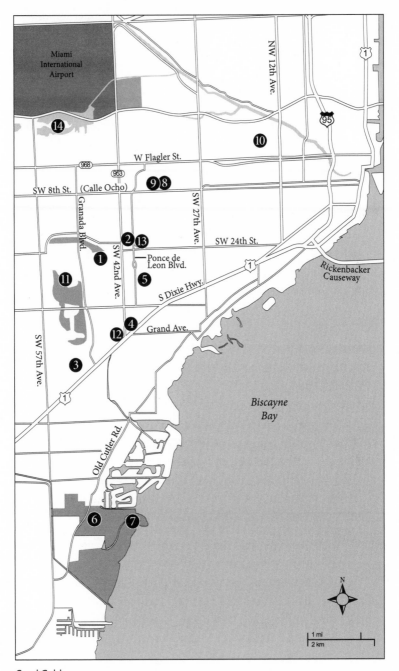

Coral Gables

university, but there's also a magnificent tropical garden and 2 lovely locations to take your children for a swim.

One of the most kid-oriented attractions in Coral Gables is the glorious Venetian Pool. This 820,000 gallon swimming hole was created in 1923 out of a coral rock quarry. Italian-style loggias and porticos, along with caves, waterfalls, palm trees, and a bridge, were added. Today the Venetian Pool remains a spectacular place to swim. The clear, pristine water feels chilly, because it's fed by a spring, so this experience is best enjoyed on a hot day. Children have fun exploring the nooks and crannies of this popular site. A separate, shallow pool makes it easier to keep an eye on little ones. Lifeguards watch over swimmers. Children must be 3 years old and 38 inches tall to enter; if your 3-year-old stands under 38 inches, you'll need to provide proof of his or her age. A concession stand selling sandwiches, drinks, and snacks is open in summer. On summer weekends, the pool can grow very crowded.

Venetian Pool
2701 De Soto Blvd., Coral Gables 33134
305.460.5306
http://www.coralgables.com
Until October 28: adults $11.50, children (3–12) $6.60
October 29 to November 30: adults $7.70, children (3–12) $4.15
Closed December, January, and major holidays
Tuesday through Friday 11:00 a.m. to 5:30 p.m., Saturday through Sunday 10:00 a.m. to 4:30 p.m. (Hours change throughout the year. Check website or call to confirm.)
Ages: M, TW, TN

If all that swimming makes your family hungry, dry off and drive over to Miracle Mile, the main strip for dining and shopping. This commercial street (also known as Coral Way) dates from 1922 and runs from LeJeune Road (a.k.a. 42nd Avenue)

Coral Gables has its own style, even for its street signs.
Photo by Zickie Allgrove.

to Douglas Road (37th Avenue). In front of Coral Gables City Hall at the corner of Miracle Mile and LeJeune you'll see a large statue of George Merrick himself. For 90 years, families have strolled down Miracle Mile, and there are still places to eat, shops to browse, and a theater, both on the Mile and nearby streets Ponce de Leon Boulevard and Aragon Avenue. (See the Restaurants section for specific recommendations.) In our era of gigantic shopping malls, Miracle Mile with its small storefronts may strike visitors as quaint. Pleasant, yes, but no longer truly miraculous.

Children's stores include Boy Meets Girl, with luxe clothing and shoes (355 Miracle Mile); Peace Love World, with kids' clothes (225 Miracle Mile); Barnes and Noble, with children's books and toys and a large Spanish book selection (152 Miracle Mile); and Bellini, selling high-end children's furniture (50 Miracle Mile). Other shops will interest the adults, like Luminaire, Sabor Havana Cigars, and Klein Jeweler's.

✸ NECESSITIES

If you need Band-Aids, diaper ointment, or other sundries, Navarro Discount Pharmacy is located at 93 Miracle Mile (305.445.1059). For organic and gluten-free snacks, there's a Whole Foods Market close to the University of Miami at 6701 Red Road (305.421.9421).

Throughout the year, the Actors' Playhouse at the historic Miracle Theater presents musicals for children. Past performances have included *Peter Rabbit and the Garden of Doom*, *Cinderella*, and *A Christmas Carol*; these usually take place on Saturday afternoons. You can purchase tickets and select seats online; prices for the children's shows run from approximately $19.50 to $22.50. Their performance schedule along with descriptions of the musicals is available online.

Actors' Playhouse at the Miracle Theater
280 Miracle Mile
Coral Gables 33134
305.444.4181
http://www.actorsplayhouse.org
Ages: B/T, M, TW (Depending on the production)

One block north of Miracle Mile is the most famous bookstore in town, Books and Books. Housed in a historic Spanish-style building with an agreeable courtyard café, this independent bookstore has hosted some of the most famous writers in the world. One wing of the store is home to a great children and teenagers' section; occasionally children's book authors give readings, so check the website for current events. Saturdays at 10:00 a.m. the store hosts a story time for children aged 3 to 7. On Friday nights there's live music in the courtyard. Families make a night of buying books, eating dinner, and listening to the tunes. (There is not a children's menu, however.) The shop also has outposts in South Beach, Bal Harbour, the Miami International Airport, and Grand Cayman.

Books and Books
265 Aragon Ave.
Coral Gables 33134
305.442.4408
http://www.booksandbooks.com
Sunday through Thursday 9:00 a.m. to 11:00 p.m., Friday and Satur-
    day 9:00 a.m. to 12:00 midnight

⊘ SURVIVAL TIP

Street parking can be hard to come by on Miracle Mile. If you're not having luck, go 1 block north to Aragon Avenue, where you will find pay parking lots as well as a parking garage situated next to the Coral Gables Art Cinema (260 Aragon) and across the street from Books and Books.

History buffs curious about Coral Gables may want to visit Merrick House, the family home of George Merrick, founder of Coral Gables. (It's also known as the Coral Gables Merrick House.) His parents were among the early settlers of Miami, and the charming 1906 bungalow, built of oolite limestone (coral rock), displays many of their furnishings and vintage possessions. (To give a sense of how small the Miami community was in the early 1900s: George Merrick eventually married Eunice Peacock, granddaughter of Charles and Isabella Peacock, who built Miami's first hotel in Coconut Grove.) The Merrick House is open 2 days a week, and the tour lasts 45 minutes.

Merrick House
907 Coral Way
Coral Gables 33134
305.460.5093
Adults $5, children (6–12) $1, children 5 and under free
Wednesdays and Sundays only, tours at 1:00 p.m., 2:00 p.m., and
    3:00 p.m.
Ages: M, TW, TN

The recently opened Coral Gables Museum exemplifies the best of Coral Gables' devotion to history and preservation. Housed in the city's original Police and Fire Station as well as new buildings, this institution features exhibits designed to appeal to children and adults, and focuses on local history, design, and architecture. The second Saturday of each month the museum hosts the free-of-charge "Family Day on Aragon" from 11:00 a.m. to 4:00 p.m., with craft making, music, storytelling, and movie matinees. Conveniently located next to Books and Books and one block from Miracle Mile.

Coral Gables Museum
285 Aragon Ave.
Coral Gables 33134
305.603.8067
http://www.coralgablesmuseum.org
Tuesday through Thursday 12:00 noon to 6:00 p.m., Saturday 11:00
a.m. to 5:00 p.m., Sunday 12:00 noon to 5:00 p.m., closed Mondays
Adults $7, children (6–12) $3, children under 6 free
Ages: B/T, M, TW, TN

A drive through Coral Gables gives you an overview of how the city maintains its architectural purity, from the lovingly restored Mediterranean Revival homes to office high-rises with incongruous red-tile roofs. From Miracle Mile, take Ponce de Leon Boulevard north and turn left on Alhambra. Follow Alhambra across LeJeune Road and continue until you reach Granada. Turn left. Follow Granada south past the golf course. Situated amid tropical gardens and behind banyan trees are pastel mansions. You'll circle an impressive roundabout (traffic circle) with a fountain at Desoto Boulevard, just near the Venetian Pool. The Biltmore Hotel appears majestically in the distance. You can keep driving south on Granada until you reach Bird Road (SW 40th Street), which is the end of this driving tour. Here, if you turn left, you'll soon be at LeJeune Road. From the corner of Bird and LeJeune, head north (left) if you want to return to Miracle Mile. South (or right) will take you to U.S. 1 (South Dixie Highway).

African art at the Lowe Art Museum. Courtesy of
the Lowe Art Museum, University of Miami.

🌧 RAINY DAY

When thunderstorms threaten to deluge Coral Gables, drive over
to the beautifully landscaped University of Miami and its Lowe Art
Museum. If your children haven't visited an art museum before,
the Lowe will give them an accessible introduction with its manageable size and range of work. The Lowe has a small permanent
collection with art from Europe, including a Monet painting and
a 4th century Greek krater (mixing bowl). Their Asian collection
ranges from a Chinese Tang Dynasty horse to feisty Korean Lion-
Dogs. The Lowe's galleries also display art of the Americas, Africa,
and the Pacific Islands, along with changing exhibitions. There are
restrooms and a gift shop. Metered parking is available.

Lowe Art Museum
1301 Stanford Dr.
Coral Gables 33124
305.284.3535
http://www.miami.edu/lowe

Adults $10, children under 12 free, students (with ID card) $5
Tuesday through Saturday 10:00 a.m. to 4:00 p.m., Sunday 12:00
noon to 4:00 p.m., closed Mondays and holidays
Ages: M, TW, TN

More Coral Gables shopping can be found at the Village of Merrick Park, a high-end, 3-story plaza built around a large outdoor courtyard with palm trees and a fountain. Neiman Marcus and Nordstrom anchor the development; children's shops include Janie and Jack and Pottery Barn Kids. For adults, there is Banana Republic, Anthropologie, L'Occitane, Gucci, Coach, A Pea in the Pod, Tommy Bahama, and Burberry.

The Village of Merrick Park sees lots of families; some mothers and grandmothers may have Chanel bags casually draped over their shoulders, but the display of wealth is usually low-key. (Except when someone's valet parking a lime green Maserati.) Plenty of folks of ordinary means enjoy Merrick Park's shops and easy parking, too. You have a selection of restaurants to choose from: Nordstrom Café Bistro (see Restaurants section), C'est Bon sandwich shop, CG Burgers and Pizza, Mariposa at

After lunch, children and parents take time to run around at the lushly landscaped Village of Merrick Park. Photo by Zickie Allgrove.

Neiman Marcus, the Italian eatery Villagio, Asian fusion and sushi at SAWA, the American bistro CRAVE, and Yard House.

The Village of Merrick Park
358 San Lorenzo Ave.
Coral Gables 33146
305.529.0200
http://www.villageofmerrickpark.com
Monday through Saturday 10:00 a.m. to 9:00 p.m., Sunday 12:00
noon to 6:00 p.m.

✳ DEAL

The Coral Gables Trolley stops outside the Village of Merrick Park, on the traffic circle near its Ponce de Leon Avenue entrance. This free trolley bus drives through the center of Coral Gables; it connects to the Douglas Road Metrorail Station and also stops at Miracle Mile. It runs only on weekdays, from 6:30 a.m. to 8:00 p.m. A no-cost excursion for kids who like watching the world from a trolley window.

If you'd rather embrace the great outdoors than shop, the southeast section of Coral Gables—hugging Biscayne Bay—has 2 of Miami's best-known nature attractions. The first, Fairchild Tropical Botanic Garden, showcases a huge, lush tropical landscape with various exhibits: Windows to the Tropics (orchids, bromeliads, ferns, etc.), a palmetum, a rainforest, butterfly garden, arboretum, succulent section, and Keys coastal habitat. Born in 1869, David Fairchild was a botanist who traveled the world and introduced over 200,000 crops and plants to America. He and his wife built a house called "The Kampong" in Coconut Grove in 1926 and became part of the community. Fairchild Garden was named in his honor (by his friend Colonel Montgomery), and many plants here were gathered by David Fairchild himself.

The narrated tram tour is a must. You'll learn many entertaining facts, such as why the peeling gumbo limbo is called the "tourist tree" and which plant is endearingly known as "Mr. Stinky." Depending on the tour guide, you may also hear some ear-bending puns. Kids often enjoy the shaded tram ride, and it gives everyone's feet a rest. The tram stops at the Lakeside Cafe, serving hot dogs, sandwiches, panini, quiche, and salads. The Glass House Café, located across from the rainforest, is decorated with sculptor Dale Chihuly's extravagant glass chandelier. The menu features items such as the Mediterranean wrap and the Asian mango chicken salad.

Toddlers and older children have acres to run around on, without the worry of traffic. Teenagers who are interested in nature may appreciate the gardens; other teens may gripe that perennial teenage gripe, "I'm bored." There are restrooms and a gift store with children's books and toys. In summer and fall Fairchild occasionally offers free days; the best way to find exact dates is by looking on their website or calling.

~~~~~~

Fairchild Tropical Botanic Garden
10901 Old Cutler Rd.
Coral Gables 33156
305.667.1651
http://www.fairchildgarden.org
Adults $25, children (6–17) $12, children 5 and under free
Monday through Friday 9:30 a.m. to 4:30 p.m., Saturday and Sunday 7:30 a.m. to 4:30 p.m.
Ages: B/T, M, TW, TN

~~~~~~

The second nature attraction, quite close by, is Matheson Hammock Park and Beach. "Hammock" refers not to the mesh sling you might hook up between 2 trees but to the tropical forests of hardwoods, palms, and exotic shrubs that once covered much of south Florida. Parts of Matheson Hammock Park and Beach indeed appear wooded and natural. The beach area exudes a family-friendly vibe with a man-made atoll pool, which

Even kids can learn to windsurf at Matheson Hammock Park.
Courtesy of Adventure Sports Miami.

connects to the bay. Its protected, extremely calm waters make it ideal for taking a dip with babies and toddlers. (Teenagers, on the other hand, may prefer the water sports options close by.) There are restrooms and nature trails in the park. The restaurant, Red Fish Grill, is only open for dinner. Adventure Sports Miami rents kayaks, standup paddleboards, and kiteboarding equipment at the park. Lessons for children can also be arranged. The company posts weather updates online; or you can call in advance to check water and wind conditions. One hour of SUP rental plus a lesson costs $35 (305.733.1519 or http://www.adventuresportsmiami.com).

Matheson Hammock Park and Beach
9610 Old Cutler Rd.
Coral Gables 33156
305.665.5475
$5 per car weekdays, $6 per car weekends
Open sunrise to sunset
Ages: B/T, M, TW, TN

Little Havana

East of Coral Gables, Little Havana is the neighborhood that in the 1960s grew to be populated mainly by Cubans who had fled the communist Castro regime. It is one of the most Spanish-speaking areas in all of Miami. Older Cuban men smack down dominos in heated games at Domino Park. Little window-front coffee shops serve piping hot *cortaditos* and milky Cuban *café con leches*. Botánicas run by *santeras* and *santeros* sell statues and colored beads for those who worship the orishas. (Although the statues may appear to be Catholic saints, in fact the orishas originated from the Yoruba people in Africa. Each orisha—or god—has his or her own colors, songs, offerings, and dances.) Flags of Cuba and murals of Cuban scenery proliferate. The main artery of Little Havana is 8th Street, more commonly known as Calle Ocho (pronounced cah-yay o-cho).

Today, immigrants from Central American countries live side-by-side with Cubans. Visitors who come to Little Havana looking for a tourist experience could be disappointed; it's primarily a place where people live and work. The architecture bears no resemblance to the graceful colonial mansions found in La Habana Vieja in Cuba. Stores on Calle Ocho sit squished together in utilitarian blocks. Nevertheless, Cuban culture can be sampled at the Little Havana Cigar Factory (1501 SW 8th Street) with its hand-rolled cigars. Artisanal frozen treats will tempt the family at Azucar Ice Cream Company (1503 SW 8th Street). To shop for traditional linen guayaberas (dress shirts) and Cuban souvenirs, visit Sentir Cubano (3100 SW 8th Street).

♀ INSIDE SCOOP

Parents who want to taste the real Little Havana should stop by one of the tiny storefronts selling strong Cuban-style coffee. A *café con leche* is espresso coffee served with warm milk and sugar. (Say "sin azucar" if you don't want it sweetened.) A *cafecito* is a thimble-sized shot of espresso. (With sugar, of course.) A *colada* is a bigger cup of the same coffee, usually served with little tiny cups—so you can share. It's that strong! A *cortadito* is like a *café con leche*, but with less milk. After drinking, you should have plenty of energy to keep up with the kids.

The best way to get a feel for Little Havana is to have breakfast at Miami institution Versailles (pronounced ver-sigh-yeahs). Although you can try a meal in the ornately decorated restaurant, going next door to the bakery will put you right into the thick of things. To be authentic, order a *café con leche* or espresso with guava pastries (*pasteles de guayaba*) or buttered Cuban toast. Be prepared to try a little Spanish or simply point and smile.

Versailles
3501 SW 8th St.
Miami 33135
305.441.2500
http://www.versailles-bakery.com

Calle Ocho (8th Street) has other types of cuisine besides the classic Cuban; see the Restaurants section for Mexican and Asian recommendations.

Cuban guayaberas, those lightweight traditional shirts with pleats and pockets, remain a popular Miami souvenir for men. If you drive west a little over 2 miles, you'll come to one of the best-known guayabera stores in America, Ramon Puig. Here the practical, cotton-polyester blend short-sleeve shirts run from about $40. The deluxe version, in Irish linen with long sleeves, goes for about $150, and is the epitome of Old World tropical elegance. (Perfect for cocktails at the exclusive Miramar Yacht Club in pre-Castro Havana.) Everyone from Ernest Hemingway to Ronald Reagan wore a Ramon Puig creation. Mr. Puig, "the King of Guayaberas," opened his store in Cuba in 1943; today his family maintains the tradition, while adding versions in new colors. 5840 SW 8th Street, Miami 33144, 1.855.GUAYABERA, http://www.ramonpuig.com.

♀ INSIDE SCOOP

Little Havana holds Viernes Culturales or "Cultural Fridays" the last Friday of every month. During these events Calle Ocho becomes somewhat more accessible for visiting tourists, with cigar rollers demonstrating their technique, art galleries staying open into the evening, and salsa and tango dancing. Some venues have live music, and a local historian gives a free tour. You can look on their website or telephone to confirm what will be featured on the upcoming Cultural Friday, if one takes place during your trip. The main activities are centered on SW 8th Street between 14th and 17th avenues, from 7:00 to 11:00 p.m. the last Friday each month.

Viernes Culturales
1637 SW 8th St.
Miami 33135
305.643.5500
http://www.viernesculturales.org

In north Little Havana you'll find the new Marlins Park, a stunning, LEED-certified retractable-roof ballpark and home to the Miami Marlins baseball team. From late February spring training through the regular season in September, you and your kids have the chance to see Miami's home team go toe-to-toe with all the Major League ball clubs—sometimes in air-conditioned comfort. Parking can be reserved online in advance (a smart strategy). Cheap seats can go for about $27 (sometimes even less), while the best seats can cost hundreds of dollars. The Marlins' website encourages you to buy tickets online at http://www.stubhub.com or call 1.877.MARLINS. The ballpark sells a range of food, from burgers and pizza to Cuban and Mexican.

Marlins Park
501 Marlins Way (NW 16th Ave.)
Miami 33125
305.480.1300
http://www.miami.marlins.mlb.com
Ages: M, TW, TN

Restaurants

In addition to the restaurants detailed below, on Miracle Mile you will find these chains: California Pizza Kitchen (300 Miracle Mile), Cold Stone Creamery (261), Einstein Brothers Bagels (202), Starbucks (200), Panera (137), and Denny's (1). The Village of Merrick Park has several restaurants not described below, from the sandwich shop C'est Bon to Neiman Marcus's fine-dining spot, Mariposa.

💰 SPLURGE

If your children love nothing better than a fancy tea party, take them to high tea in the Biltmore Hotel's gracious lobby. The lobby's birds in their birdcage are a child magnet. The venerable grande dame of Miami hotels, this elegant establishment has been attracting visitors since 1926. Afternoon tea is served at 3:00 and 4:30 p.m. in a luxurious setting with live classical guitar music; the cost is approximately $22 per person, not including tax and tip. Reservations recommended. Biltmore Hotel and Resort, 1200 Anastasia Ave., Coral Gables 33134, 855.311.6903, http://www.biltmorehotel.com

EL REY DE LAS FRITAS

1821 SW 8th St., Miami 33135 (Little Havana), 305.644.6054

This dive-y restaurant in Little Havana specializes in the *frita*, which consists of a chorizo (Spanish sausage) patty, little fried shoestring potatoes, special sauce, and onions on a bun. A fabulous grease-fest! Also available are exotic fruit juices. Staff may speak only a little English.

HAVANA HARRY'S

4612 LeJeune Rd., Coral Gables 33146, 305.661.2622, http://www.havanaharrys.net

Havana Harry's wins a loyal following by serving excellent Cuban dishes in a casually elegant dining room. You may want to try *mariquitas* (fried plantain chips), a soup of *frijoles negros* (black beans), the Cuban sandwich, *palomilla* steak, or classic *vaca frita*.

For kids who prefer American fare, there are hamburger sliders and a grilled chicken sandwich. Prices are reasonable.

JOHN MARTIN'S IRISH PUB AND RESTAURANT

253 Miracle Mile, Coral Gables 33134, 305.445.3777, http://www. johnmartins.com

Not every pub is family-friendly, but this locals' favorite offers a children's menu and a variety of seafood and pub fare for adults. Some evenings there is live music. Open 7 days a week for lunch and dinner. Friday night happy hours can become hectic.

LA PROVENCE

2300 Ponce de Leon Blvd., Coral Gables 33134, 305.476.0530, http:// www.laprovencemiami.com

Two blocks north of Miracle Mile, La Provence sells French bread, chocolate croissants, and mouth-watering pastries. Stop in for a snack or get a breakfast bite to go.

MI RICONCITO MEXICANO

1961 SW 8th St., Miami 33135 (Little Havana), 305.644.4015

Authentic, flavorsome Mexican dishes are well priced in this family-run place. Daily specials along with tacos, quesadillas, flautas, and other dishes keep customers coming back for more.

MR. YUM

1945 SW 8th St., Miami 33135 (Little Havana), 786.360.2371, http:// www.mryummiami.com

Mr. Yum is a chicly decorated establishment that serves nicely prepared and presented Thai and Japanese food. Lunch specials such as red curry or the sushi/sashimi combo are reasonable at about $10.95.

NORDSTROM CAFE BISTRO

4310 Ponce de Leon Blvd., Coral Gables 33146, 786.999.1313, http:// www.nordstrom.com

Nordstrom's restaurant has a children's menu with well-priced meals, including mac and cheese, grilled cheese, pizza, chicken fingers, and pasta. Yummy adult dishes range from niçoise salad with salmon to roast chicken *pommes frites*. Located on the 3rd floor inside Nordstrom.

TALAVERA

2299 Ponce de Leon Blvd., Coral Gables 33134, 305.444.2955, http://www.talaveraspot.com

This high-style Mexican restaurant serves delicious regional dishes and uses fresh, high-quality ingredients. Rich moles, fish or chicken in the "huarache grill" manner, cactus salad, and quesadillas on home-made corn tortillas are just a few of the items on their extensive menu. For its refined cooking and trendy atmosphere, Talavera has become a Coral Gables favorite.

Accommodations

Hotels here are often handy for those who wish to be close to the University of Miami, the airport, or downtown Coral Gables. If your priority in visiting Miami is beach time, Coral Gables is not especially convenient. However, for those who love golf and tennis, the Biltmore Hotel may be an ideal if expensive option.

When plans necessitate your staying near Coral Gables, but the prices seem too steep, check out hotels near the airport, such as the Sofitel listed below. Many of the major chains have rooms for 2 adults and 2 children priced around $100 to $120. (The downside will be the traffic, particularly during rush hour.)

BILTMORE HOTEL

1200 Anastasia Ave., Coral Gables 33134, 855.311.6903, http://www.biltmorehotel.com

This impressive historic property is famous for Old World refinement. It has golf, tennis, a beautiful pool, a fitness center, and a spa. Their Palme d'Or is a top-rated French restaurant; Fontana serves Italian in an outdoor courtyard; and Cascade is poolside. For children, there are spa treatments, junior golf clinics, tennis lessons, and Biltmore Buddies (a drop-off activity program for kids with rates from $25 to $55 per child). Advance purchase room rates for 2 adults and 2 children can be found for $236, while regular rates start at $359. Check the website for specials and discounts.

SOFITEL MIAMI

5800 Blue Lagoon Dr., Miami 33126, 305.264.4888, http://www.sofitel. com

The Sofitel is one of the chain hotels located a few miles from— but *not in*—Coral Gables, just next to the Miami airport. A room here for 2 adults and 2 children runs about $115 on internet travel sites such as http://www.expedia.com or http://www. kayak.com. The business-oriented Sofitel has an outdoor pool with waterfall, fitness center, restaurant, and free airport shuttle. If your budget is tight, airport hotels often offer good value, but keep in mind that all Miami attractions will be a decent drive away.

WESTIN COLONNADE, CORAL GABLES

180 Aragon Ave., Coral Gables 33134, 305.441.2600, http://www. westincoralgables.com

The Westin has an attractive pool deck on its roof, a fitness center, and 24-hour room service; children under 17 stay free. A room with 2 double beds starts at $209 for 2 adults and 2 kids. Its location on Aragon and Miracle Mile puts you in walking distance to restaurants, shops, and the theater. This property would make particular sense if business brings you or your spouse to Coral Gables and your family has accompanied you.

Southern Miami

People often refer to the suburbs south of Miami as "south Miami." But this can lead to some confusion, because there is a small *township* also named South Miami located west of Coral Gables. Whatever you choose to call them, the southern Miami suburbs contain miles of houses with red tile roofs and Mediterranean architecture. Landscapes of bright green lawns and graceful royal palms with gray trunks create a tranquil, tropical environment. In contrast to this lush tranquility are the highly trafficked main arteries brimming with "big box" stores and strip malls that make up the neighborhoods of Kendall, Perrine, Pinecrest, Cutler Bay, and Country Walk, flanked on the southeast side by Biscayne Bay and on the western side by the Everglades. Tucked among these residential enclaves are special spots including popular children's attractions and an eccentric coral rock castle.

Driving past mile after mile of tiled-roof homes and perfectly clipped grass, you'd be forgiven for thinking that nothing out of

Tropical hibiscus flowers grow in southern Miami and throughout the region. Photo by Laura Albritton.

the ordinary ever occurred—that nothing unexpected or exotic ever ruffled the palm fronds of the carefully tended gardens. But there you'd be wrong!

Decades ago, a place called the Rare Bird Farm in Kendall imported a few Red-whiskered Bulbul birds from Calcutta, India. Bulbuls are songbirds, and their habitat stretches from Africa to the Middle East all the way to Indonesia. They certainly do not make their nests in North or South America. Yet, there were the Red-whiskered Bulbuls, living out their lives quietly and anonymously on a bird farm in a Miami suburb. But in the 1960s, some of these clever little critters escaped from their aviary.

Apparently, the bulbuls really, really liked Kendall, preferring it to South Beach, Coconut Grove, or Key Biscayne. Because these Indian birds have remained exclusively in this small, fairly unremarkable portion of Miami, populating the trees and thickets with their young. Yes, other sections of Miami remain tragically

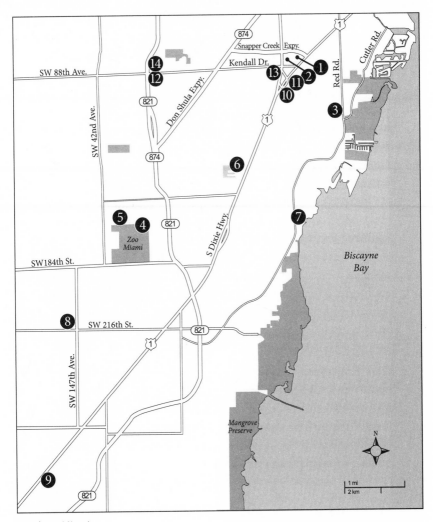

Southern Miami

Map Key

1. Dadeland North Metrorail Station
2. Dadeland Mall
3. Pinecrest Gardens
4. Zoo Miami
5. Gold Coast Railroad Museum
6. The Falls
7. The Deering Estate at Cutler
8. Monkey Jungle
9. Coral Castle Museum
10. Anthony's Pizza
11. Captain's Tavern Restaurant & Seafood Market
12. La Carreta
13. Hotel Indigo
14. Country Inn & Suites Kendall

bulbul-free. Should you try to spot one: they have black pointy heads or crests and small red patches next to their eyes.

The nearby Village of Pinecrest had an entirely different sort of distinguished foreign visitor. In 1936 Mr. and Mrs. Scherr opened Parrot Jungle, an attraction with parrots and other feathered fowl; entrance back then was only 25¢. At first only about 100 people came, but soon word spread and the crowds gathered. In 1946 they welcomed none other than Sir Winston Churchill, victorious after World War II but no longer prime minister of Britain.

There is a wonderful black-and-white photograph of Sir Winston, with cane and cigar, posing beside an amorous-looking cockatoo and an indignant macaw. Since the glory days, Parrot Jungle has moved (and is now Jungle Island near South Beach) and the pleasant park that remains in Pinecrest no longer lures in the great and the good. Nonetheless, southern Miami still has more than a few amusing entertainments up its sleeve.

⊘ SURVIVAL TIP

During rush hour, the drive to southern Miami's attractions can be lengthy if you're coming from the beach, Coconut Grove, or Key Biscayne. Miami has grown north and south in a long strip, which means getting from the north or central end to the south can be time-consuming. On Sunday mornings, though, the roads are generally free of heavy traffic.

RAINY DAY

When you need to escape the rain while in southern Miami, Dadeland Mall offers the classic American mall experience, with plenty of shopping and chain restaurants. It's located in Kendall, in the northern section of southern Miami. Macy's, Saks Fifth Avenue, Nordstrom, Apple, J.Crew, Disney, Abercrombie and Fitch, Kid's Foot Locker, and Michael Kors rub shoulders with plenty of other stores. The food court has Asian, Latin, and American fast food; the mall also contains a Cheesecake Factory and a Villagio Italian restaurant. The Metrorail stops at Dadeland South, a few blocks away.

Dadeland Mall
7535 N. Kendall Dr.
Miami 33156
305.665.6227
http://www.simon.com/mall/dadeland-mall

DEAL

Steep admission prices can become the bane of a vacation. Approximately 3 miles from Dadeland Mall is the inexpensive Pinecrest Gardens. Tropical plants, palm trees, and hardwood forest make this an urban oasis. Toddlers and small children have a blast in the Splash 'N Play area; it's open from 10:00 a.m. The playground is open all day and the petting zoo opens at 10:00 a.m., 12:00 noon, 2:00 p.m., and 4:00 p.m. You can buy food to feed the fish. "Swan Lake" features a swan, turtles, and iguanas. See the website for upcoming movies, dance performances, and plays including Miami Children's Theater shows. (Pinecrest Gardens is the site of the former Parrot Jungle, now *sans* parrots.)

Pinecrest Gardens
11000 Red Rd.
Pinecrest 33156
305.669.6990
http://www.pinecrest-fl.gov
Adults $3, children (3–17) $2, children with Splash 'N Play Pass $3, children 2 and under free
Fall and winter 9:00 a.m. to 5:00 p.m., Spring and summer 9:00 a.m. to 6:00 p.m.
Ages: B/T, M

For many more exotic animals (around 700!) drive approximately 10 miles from either Dadeland Mall or Pinecrest Gardens to Zoo Miami. The well-maintained facilities feature lions, tigers, elephants, zebras, chimpanzees, ostriches, and koalas, to name just a few. Zoo exhibits sprawl over many acres, up and down paths planted with flowers and leafy shrubs. The park is divided into African, Asian, and Australian sections. Zoo Miami

Zoo Miami's Wacky Barn gives children a chance to get up close to animals.
Courtesy of Zoo Miami.

is developing large-scale exhibits for the Everglades. The new Amazon and Beyond showcases amazing creatures from Central and South America. Gardens, aviaries, and a children's petting zoo round out the property. Check the schedule at the entrance for daily presentations with zookeepers.

The Children's Zoo is just one section of the overall zoo property. Here you'll find the funny-shaped Wacky Barn with farm animals; the Toadstool, with geckos and cavefish; the Meerkat exhibit; Humpey's Camel Rides, which cost $5; a wildlife carousel; and a butterfly garden. Zoo Miami has stroller and wheelchair rentals, as well as a Monorail with 4 stops, a tram tour, and Safari Cycles that you can pedal to get around. These each cost additional fees. On hot summer days when the zoo's paths feel extremely long, a Safari Cycle starts to look very appealing. The Pink Flamingo, Carousel Cafe, Oasis Cafe, and Fiesta Grille serve snacks and quick meals. The handy map, given out at the entrance, points out where several restrooms are located throughout the park. The shuttle service Zoo Miami Express takes tourists from their hotels to the zoo, for a cost of $65 per adult and $55 per child 10 and under, which includes zoo admission (http://www.zoomiamiexpress.com, 786.350.7036).

Zoo Miami

1 Zoo Blvd.

12400 SW 152nd St.

Miami 33177

305.251.0400

http://www.miamimetrozoo.com

Adults $15.95 + tax, children (3–12) $11.95 + tax, children 2 and under free

9:30 a.m. to 5:30 p.m. 365 days a year (ticket booth closes at 4:30 p.m.)

Ages: B/T, M, TW

The Gold Coast Railroad Museum is just near the zoo and gives adults and kids the chance to learn about railroads and also ride trains. The collection includes locomotives, freight cars, and passenger cars, not least of which is a presidential railcar. The Edwin Link Children's Railroad runs on a 2-foot track on the weekends and costs $3 per person. Standard gauge trains with diesel locomotives run some weekends and cost $6 per person. If you plan on visiting on a weekday, call ahead to see if any of the trains will be in operation. During the year a full-sized Thomas Train visits the museum; check the website for upcoming events. The museum displays a collection of model trains and also has wooden train sets that children can play with.

Gold Coast Railroad Museum

12450 SW 152nd St.

Miami, FL 33177

305.253.0063

http://www.gcrm.org

Adults $6, children 3–12 $4, children 2 and under free

Train rides $2.50, $6, $12, depending on the train

Monday through Friday 10:00 a.m. to 4:00 p.m., Saturday and Sunday 11:00 a.m. to 4:00 p.m. (model train building open until 2:00 p.m.)

Ages: B/T, M, TW, TN

Near both the zoo and the railroad museum is a Walgreens drugstore at 15255 SW 137 Avenue (305.233.8499). Close to Dadeland Mall is the 24-hour CVS Pharmacy at 8765 S. Dixie Highway (305.740.6840).

Some folks love malls; others hate them. If you're in the latter category, at least at The Falls (about 4 miles from the zoo) you'll be able to wander outdoors and enjoy attractive tropical plantings, pleasant fountains, and covered walkways. The outside setting makes it an easy place to stroll with kids. Child-oriented stores include the American Girl Doll store, Disney, Build-A-Bear Workshop, Gap Kids, and Justice. Among other shops are Bloomingdale's, Apple, Macy's, Crate and Barrel, and Vera Bradley. There is a movie theater along with several chain restaurants: TGI Fridays, Crepemaker, Häagen-Dazs, Johnny Rockets, Los Ranchos, P. F. Chang's, and Red Robin.

The Falls
8888 SW 136th St.
Miami 33176
305.255.4571
http://www.simon.com/mall/the-falls

In 1913 an industrialist named Charles Deering from Chicago made his mark in southern Miami. He was the brother of James Deering, who built Vizcaya, and the son of William Deering of the Deering Harvester Company, and he had pots of money. Initially, he bought a wood-frame hotel, Richmond Cottage, overlooking the keyhole-shaped boat basin on the shores of Biscayne Bay and transformed it into his home. Then, like his brother, he ordered up a Mediterranean Revival mansion (the Stone House). This was where Deering displayed his art collection of Goyas, Rembrandts, and El Grecos.

The famous paintings no longer hang in the Stone House, and not as many furnishings are on display as at Vizcaya, so that the

Richmond Cottage and the Stone House at the Deering Estate.
Courtesy of the Deering Estate at Cutler. Photo by Brian F. Call.

interiors strike you as understated by comparison. What makes
the Deering Estate extraordinary are the 444 unspoiled acres of
nature that Deering cherished and that subsequent generations
have preserved. Mangrove forests, hardwood hammock, salt
marshes, and coastal flora thrive in this protected park. Endangered plants survive and serve as habitat to wildlife and native
birds.

Tours of Stone House, with its limestone-veneered walls and
hand-carved columns, and of Richmond Cottage are led by a naturalist at 10:30 a.m. and 3:00 p.m. From October through May a
guide leads a tour of the nature areas at 12:30 p.m. A new raised
walkway takes you next to the Cutler Burial Mound, where 12 to
18 Tequesta Indians lie buried in a circle. What you will actually
see is a magnificent, 350-year-old oak atop . . . a forested mound
of earth. Its secrets remain hidden from view, just as it should
be. Other specialty tours including kayaking and canoe trips cost
extra and must be arranged in advance. For ambling, picnicking,
birding, and getting away from the city's throngs, the Deering

Estate is lovely. Not the place, however, if your family's seeking nonstop, thrill-a-minute excitement.

The Deering Estate at Cutler
16701 SW 72nd Ave.
Miami 33157
305.235.1668
http://www.deeringestate.com
10:00 a.m. to 5:00 p.m. 7 days a week except Thanksgiving and Christmas (box offices closes at 4:00 p.m.)
Adults $12, children (4–14) $7, children 3 and under free
Ages: M, TW, TN

Even further south, on the opposite (western) side of S. Dixie Highway, sits Monkey Jungle, a vintage Miami attraction with primates such as squirrel monkeys, macaques, lemurs, capuchins, and a gorilla. At scheduled times throughout the day, there are feedings and staff presentations at the Monkey Swimming Pool, the Amazonian Rain Forest, and with the orangutans. In some sections, human beings are fenced or caged in a tunnel-like space so that the monkeys have more freedom of movement. Some visitors—especially little ones—love the emphasis on monkeys and don't mind the somewhat dated displays; other guests complain that there's not enough to see, given the price of admission. The park has a gift shop and snack bar.

Monkey Jungle
14805 SW 216th St.
Miami 33170
305.235.1611
http://www.monkeyjungle.com
9:30 a.m. to 5:00 p.m. 7 days a week (box office closes at 4:00 p.m.)
Adults $29.95, children (3–9) $23.95, children under 3 free
Ages: B/T, M, TW

Children who are wild about monkeys—and can't wait to interact with them one-on-one—may urge you to spring for the Rainforest Adventure. The $89.95 fee (per person) includes park admission and comes with a guided tour and monkey food. Tours are led at 10:00 a.m., 12:15 p.m., and 2:30 p.m. and require reservations (305.235.1611).

Finally, 5 miles south of Monkey Jungle, close to the city of Homestead, is the baffling Coral Castle. This roadside attraction can be a short stop-off on your way to the Keys, or as a side trip from Monkey Jungle, especially for those drawn to the weird and the wacky. The monumental shapes and walls were carved, moved, and arranged by a single Latvian man, Edward Leedskalin, over 2 decades. They stand as a testament to his love for a young woman named Agnes who (perhaps noticing Ed's somewhat obsessive streak) jilted him the night before their wedding. Coral Castle attracts its fair share of paranormal enthusiasts and has a certain kitsch appeal. If large carved blocks of coral rock don't sound like your family's thing—they're probably not.

Coral Castle Museum
28655 S. Dixie Highway
Miami 33033
305.248.6345
http://www.coralcastle.com
Adults $15, children (7–12) $7, children 6 and under free
Sunday through Thursday 8:00 a.m. to 6:00 p.m., Friday and Saturday 8:00 a.m. to 8:00 p.m.
Ages: B/T, M, TW, TN

Restaurants

Restaurants of almost every nationality can be found in the southern suburbs, often in unassuming strip malls. These suburbs are family-oriented, and the vast majority of establishments welcome children.

ANTHONY'S PIZZA

10205 S. Dixie Highway, Pinecrest 33156, 305.740.5800 and 12502 SW 88th Street, Miami 33186, 305.273.8020, http://www. anthonyscoalfiredpizza.com

This popular chain has 2 locations in southern Miami; both serve thin crust, tasty pizzas cooked in a coal-fired oven. Families make this a busy spot, particularly for dinner.

⚲ INSIDE SCOOP

CAPTAIN'S TAVERN RESTAURANT AND SEAFOOD MARKET

9625 S. Dixie Highway, Miami 33156, 305.666.5979, http://www. captainstavernmiami.com

For an old-school Florida seafood experience, complete with nautical décor, try Captain's Tavern. Regulars know to come on Tuesday nights for 2-for-1 Maine lobsters. Fresh fish, seafood, and steaks are presented in generous portions. A children's menu is available, and they have a good wine list, with several bottles under $25.

GOLDEN KRUST

9534 SW 160th St., Miami 33157, 305.256.6088, http://www. goldenkrustbakery.com

Golden Krust's Jamaican patties consist of a flaky crust that contains a warm, savory filling. Not only beef but also chicken, shrimp, and vegetable patties are served in this fast-food joint, along with other Jamaican dishes. Close to Zoo Miami and Gold Coast Railroad Museum.

IMLEE BISTRO

12663 S. Dixie Highway, Pinecrest 33156, 786.293.2223, http://www.imleeindianbistro.com

This small Indian bistro prepares many vegetarian dishes, as well as shrimp Madras curry and lamb tikka masala. Live sitar music from 7:00 p.m. on Sunday, Monday, and Tuesday nights. Open 7 days for lunch and dinner.

LA CARRETA

11740 N. Kendall Dr., Miami 33186, 305.596.5973, http://www.lacarreta.com

La Carreta is a local family-owned chain that bustles with diners who've come for Cuban comfort food in an unpretentious setting. *Arroz con pollo* (chicken with yellow rice) and the *vaca frita* (grilled shredded beef) are good choices. There are also non-Cuban items such as grilled cheese and a tuna sandwich.

SHIBUI

7101 SW 102nd Ave., Miami 33173, 305.274.5578, http://www.shibuimiami.com

This Japanese restaurant has been a locals' spot for many years. Children like sitting at the Japanese-style tables on the floor, although regular tables are available. They serve sushi, Japanese entrées, and children's dishes (fish, chicken, shrimp, etc., with rice). Open for dinner only.

Accommodations

For many tourists, it frankly does not make sense to get a hotel in southern Miami. The closest beach is Matheson Hammock in Coral Gables, about 4-and-a-half miles from Hotel Indigo and Dadeland Mall. But if you plan to do a *lot* of activities here, it might be worth spending a night.

HOTEL INDIGO

7600 N. Kendall Dr., Miami 33156, 305.595.6000, http://www.
miamidadelandhotel.com

This hotel has the hip, modern décor the Indigo chain is known for. It stands literally just off the Snapper Creek Expressway and very close to Dadeland Mall. Weekday deals start at approximately $115 a night for 2 adults and 2 children. Amenities include an outdoor pool, free Wi-Fi, free parking, free local shuttle, fitness center, Starbucks, and a bistro.

COUNTRY INN AND SUITES KENDALL

11750 Mills Dr., Miami 33183, 305.270.0359, http://www.countryinns.
com

For those seeking a bargain, this basic hotel has no-frills rooms, free breakfast, free Wi-Fi, and an outdoor pool. Internet travel sites have rates starting at $96 for 2 adults and 2 children.

9

Downtown

If you look back at the history chapter and Ralph Munroe's stunning 1884 photograph of the Miami River, it's almost impossible to grasp that the wild tropical landscape—palm trees reflecting onto still waters with a lone sailboat trailing a small dingy—has transformed into today's Downtown. Nearby Brickell, with its bright, contemporary condominiums and gleaming international banks, would be unrecognizable to the pioneering couple that neighborhood was named for. After arriving here from Ohio in 1871, William and Mary Brickell ran the only post office in Miami. Letters arrived by boat, and if Mary wasn't in a good mood, you didn't get your mail. At their trading post the Brickells snapped up alligator hides and deerskins from Seminole Indians, who arrived in dugout canoes. In return the Seminoles took sewing machines, alcohol, and beads—wares they had not previously known they needed. Mary Brickell possessed a shrewd business streak, eventually buying, selling, and developing real estate. (She sold James Deering 130 acres, where he built the massive Vizcaya in Coconut Grove.) She had great ambitions for this remote backwoods—still hardly a dot on the Florida map.

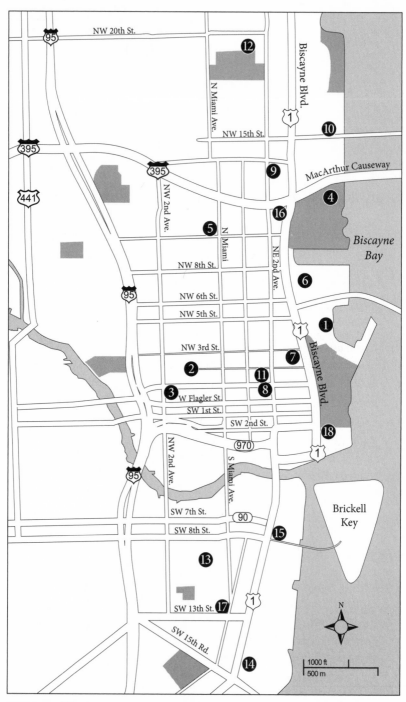

Downtown Miami

So did her contemporary, Julia Tuttle, who, in a single sale, picked up a cool 640 acres north of the Miami River. She moved from Ohio after she was widowed and began an unprecedented campaign to modernize, modernize, modernize. With an offer of free land, Tuttle enticed millionaire Henry Flagler to build a railroad to connect Miami with the rest of the civilized world. Nothing would ever be the same.

There's a statue of Tuttle in Bayfront Park. From here she surveys what Downtown Miami has become: a leading commercial hub for Latin America and the United States. The placid expression on the statue's face doesn't quite capture Julia Tuttle's wheeler-dealer tenacity.

Today's moguls keep the wheels of profit turning in the air-conditioned suites of Downtown. Hotels, corporate high-rises, and condos glisten under the sun at noon, while in the evening Downtown glows with thousands of lights. Viewed from the causeways, the sweep of skyscrapers juxtaposed against the slick surface of Biscayne Bay is absolutely striking.

From museums to music to shopping and basketball, Downtown serves up a rich cultural banquet. You'll find plenty of activities to do with children. Yet Downtown has functioned as a place principally for government and business; its transformation into an arts and entertainment hub is still ongoing. At noon sidewalks fill with office workers hurrying to their favorite lunch-time joints. In the late afternoon, one-way streets grow clogged with commuters surging home. New towers for people to work or live rise up seemingly each day. In their shadows a few historic gems, such as Freedom Tower, Trinity Episcopal

Map Key

1. Bayside Marketplace	10. Trinity Cathedral
2. Metrorail / Government Center Station	11. Gesu Catholic Church
3. HistoryMiami	12. Temple Israel of Greater Miami
4. Perez Art Museum Miami (PAMM)	13. Mary Brickell Village
5. CIFO	14. Four Season's Hotel
6. American Airlines Arena	15. Truluck's
7. CVS	16. Casa Moderna Miami
8. Olympia Theater at the Gusman Center	17. Hampton Inn Downtown and Brickell
9. The Adrienne Arsht Center	18. Intercontinental Hotel

Cathedral, and the Gusman Theater, survey all this progress. If they could speak, they might remind the shiny performing arts center and the new museum that once upon a time, they, too, were considered the very latest thing.

⊘ SURVIVAL TIP

Sections of Downtown are polished and beautifully landscaped, while certain blocks can look neglected or run-down. New galleries such as CU-1, featuring European photography (117 NE 1st Ave.), and artists' studios such as the Artisan Lounge and DWNTWN Art-House, are helping these areas evolve. On weekends and at night, some sections of Downtown can feel deserted. At these times stay oriented, park near your destination, and don't wander without a sense of where you're headed.

Also, pay close attention to the one-way streets. If you have access to the internet (or a GPS), plot your route before driving in Downtown. The street system confounds a lot of people! During large events, such as games at the American Airlines Arena, prepare for traffic jams.

At the Bayside Marketplace mall in Downtown, you can amble, shop, and eat, while savoring a view of glittering Biscayne Bay. Yes, it's touristy, with a slew of chain restaurants (see Restaurants section) and familiar chain stores such as the Gap, Victoria's Secret, the Disney Store, and Foot Locker. If you and your kids are craving mall time, this is a picturesque place to browse or have a meal. One bonus for small children is the carousel. Paid parking is available in the Bayside garage; less expensive metered parking is available across the street.

Bayside Marketplace
401 Biscayne Blvd.
Miami 33132
305.577.3344
http://www.baysidemarketplace.com
Monday through Thursday 10:00 a.m. to 10:00 p.m., Friday and Saturday 10:00 a.m. to 11:00 p.m., Sunday 11:00 a.m. to 9:00 p.m.

At Bayside Marketplace families eat, shop, and enjoy the view of Biscayne Bay. Photo by Zickie Allgrove.

Bayside Marketplace is also home to Island Queen Cruises, located near the Tradewinds Restaurant, which will take you and your children on a bilingual, 90-minute "Millionaire's Row Cruise." The boat motors by fabulous beachfront homes, Port-Miami, and Fisher Island; tours depart daily on the hour from 11:00 a.m. to 7:00 p.m. On Saturdays and Sundays the Bayside Blaster's departures take place at 11:30 a.m., 1:30 p.m., 3:30 p.m., and 5:30 p.m. Being out on the water gives you an impressive perspective on the city, not to mention the sea. Snacks and beverages are sold onboard. You can purchase tickets online at the Island Queen Cruises website, and save $3 per ticket. Then arrive 30 minutes prior to departure in order to board.

The *Island Lady* ready for a cruise at Bayside Marketplace. Photo by Zickie Allgrove.

Island Queen Cruises
Bayside Marketplace, 401 Biscayne Blvd.
Miami 33132
305.379.5119
http://www.islandqueencruises.com
Millionaire's Row Cruise: Adults $24 purchased online, $27 at the
    dock; children (4–12) $19 online, $22 at the dock
Bayside Blaster Cruise: Adults $27 purchased online, $30 at the
    dock; children (4–12) $19 online, $22 at the dock
Ages: B/T, M, TW, TN

 DEAL

The Metromover makes a stop at Bayside/College station, a few blocks west of Bayside Marketplace. The Metromover is a free, elevated people-mover that travels from the Brickell area through Downtown Miami. Cars run frequently from 5:00 a.m. to midnight in 3 separate but connecting loops, the Brickell Loop, the Inner

Loop, and the Omni Loop. Children who enjoy trains will like the bird's eye view of the city. Other stations include the Adrienne Arsht Center, Government Center (which is adjacent to HistoryMiami), and Freedom Tower.

Perhaps even more useful is the Biscayne-Brickell Trolley, which is also free. This bus, which looks like an old-fashioned trolley, travels from northern Downtown to the Brickell neighborhood, on Biscayne Boulevard and Brickell Avenue near Bayfront Park and Mary Brickell Village. It runs every 20 minutes, Monday through Saturday, 6:30 a.m. to 11:00 p.m.

HistoryMiami, a small museum and major regional archive, mounts interesting exhibitions about South Florida history and culture. Past shows include "The Guayabera," about the traditional shirt worn by Cuban and Latin American men (and still sold in Miami) and "Teen Miami." "Tropical Dreams" is the permanent exhibition that traces Miami history from prehistoric times; interactive features include a genuine historic street trolley and a model settler's house. You can park across the street at the Miami-Dade Cultural Center Parking Garage, 50 NW 2nd Avenue, or take the Metromover or Metrorail to the Government

HistoryMiami mounts exhibitions about regional history and culture. The museum also hosts free days for families. Photo by Zickie Allgrove.

Center station, then walk south across NW 1st Street. The gift shop has books, souvenirs, and various items for children. A bonus: across the plaza from the museum is the main branch of the Miami-Dade Public Library. Feel free to drop in and read one of their books to your kids in their children's section.

♀ INSIDE SCOOP

The second Saturday of each month is Family Fun Day, with free admission for all family members. From 12:00 noon to 5:00 p.m., HistoryMiami offers activities designed for children. Themed days range from "Arabic Rhythms" to "Adventures in Architecture." Themes and dates are announced on the website.

HistoryMiami
101 W. Flagler St.
305.375.1629
http://www.historymiami.org
Adults $8, children (6–12) $5, children under 6 free
Tuesday to Friday, 10:00 a.m. to 5:00 p.m., Saturday and Sunday
**   12:00 noon to 5:00 p.m., closed Mondays and holidays**
Ages: M, TW, TN

For a number of years the Miami Art Museum (MAM) existed in the same plaza as the library and HistoryMiami, but it closed after a much larger, grander facility was opened in late 2013 in the new Museum Park (formerly Bicentennial Park). Facing Biscayne Bay, the sleek Herzog and de Meuron–designed Perez Art Museum Miami (PAMM) is an impressive new landmark for the city. The museum contains 200,000 square feet of space for exhibitions of modern and contemporary art, with a library, classrooms, auditorium, workshop spaces for digital media, restaurant, and a gift shop. Special exhibits scheduled for 2014 include those of international art superstar Ai Weiwei and well-known Haitian artist Edouard Duval-Carrié. Look for installations outdoors in the Sculpture Garden. As of this writing, a bistro is scheduled to open on the first level. The first Thursday and the second Saturday of each month are free; children 12 and under always receive free admission.

Perez Art Museum Miami
1103 Biscayne Blvd.
Miami 33130
305.375.3000
http://www.pamm.org
Adults $12, youth (13–18) $6, children 12 and under free
Tuesday to Sunday, 10:00 a.m. to 6:00 p.m., additional Thursday
**   evening hours 6:00 p.m. to 9:00 p.m., closed Mondays**
Ages: M, TW, TN

Museum Park will also be the site of the impressive Patricia and Phillip Frost Museum of Science, scheduled to be completed in 2015. (For now, the Science Museum remains open in Coconut Grove.) The facility will feature an indoor "River of Grass," which will teach visitors about the Everglades; a spectacular planetarium; and the Living Core, a multifloor aquarium with sea creatures. Information on the museum and updates on its construction can be found at http://www.miasci.org.

Adventuresome kids looking for excitement will get a thrill at the Flying Trapeze School. This school, located in Bayfront Park, offers instructions on how to "fly through the air with the greatest of ease." All students wear safety harnesses, and there is always a net. Conveniently offered is a $10 "Try n' Fly," a 1-ride turn on the trapeze to see if the student wants to take a full class. Kids who love it will want to sign up for the 2-hour, $40 lesson. Children must be at least 6 years old to participate. First-timers pay a $10 registration fee. You can pay for lessons online at their website. Metered parking is found on both sides of Biscayne Boulevard, and in front of the Intercontinental Hotel. You will need to reserve your class in advance, either online or by phone.

The Flying Trapeze School
Bayfront Park
301 Biscayne Blvd.
Miami 33132
786.239.8775

http://www.theflyingtrapeze.net

Wednesday, Thursday, and Friday 7:00 to 9:00 p.m., Saturday and Sunday 4:00 to 6:00 p.m., 7:00 to 9:00 p.m.

Ages: M, TW, TN

 RAINY DAY

CIFO, or the Cisneros Fontanals Art Foundation, is one of Miami's new small museums; it houses the extraordinary art collection of Ella Fontanals-Cisneros and her family and provides grants and support for Latin American artists. The building won an AIA Design Award in 2006. Originally a 1930s warehouse, the structure was totally renovated and the front façade covered with thousands of small Bisazza tiles. Its bamboo design contrasts dramatically with the concrete used for the remainder of the space. CIFO mounts 2 main exhibitions each year; check their website to see if there is a current show (otherwise it is closed to visitors, except by appointment). Located in northern Downtown, CIFO specializes in video, photography, geometric abstraction, and other forms of contemporary work. When exhibiting, CIFO is a must-see for families who prize innovative, of-the-moment art.

CIFO
1018 N. Miami Ave.
Miami 33136
305.455.3380
http://www.cifo.org
Free admission
Thursday and Friday 12:00 noon to 6:00 p.m., Saturday and Sunday 10:00 a.m. to 4:00 p.m.*
*Museum only open during exhibition dates. Check website for upcoming and current shows.
Ages: TW, TN

Also along the bay stands the architecturally spectacular, ultramodern American Airlines Arena, designed by Miami's own Arquitectonica and 360 Architecture. Inside this white, circular building Miami fans flock to see the Miami Heat take the court against their opponents. Even if you're not a basketball follower, a Heat game is your chance to plunge into the excitement and energy of one of America's favorite sports. Regular season lasts from approximately October through April. Depending on the game, a few balcony seats will run around $17, while slightly better seats go for $68.45. (The best seats cost hundreds of dollars.) You'll find fast-food such as tacos, wraps, hot dogs, and Asian noodle bowls. Parking lots are located off NE 2nd Avenue, at 6th Street, 7th Street, 8th Street, and 9th Street; the website shows a parking map with all convenient lots laid out. The American Airlines Arena also hosts major rock and pop concerts. Purchase tickets for basketball and concerts at http://www.ticketmaster.com.

American Airlines Arena
601 Biscayne Blvd.
Miami 33132
786.777.1000
http://www.aaarena.com
Ages: M, TW, TN

If your family wants to watch football, however, it means traveling north of Miami proper to a suburb called Miami Gardens. The Sun Life Stadium is home to the famous Miami Dolphins and the University of Miami's Hurricanes. Whether you're a fan of college or pro ball, there's lots of action to be found at the 76,000 seat arena. 2269 NW 199th St., Miami Gardens 33056, 305.943.8000, http://www.sunlifestadium.com.

⚇ NECESSITIES

Very close to Bayfront Park, and near Bayside Marketplace is CVS Pharmacy. Should you need to pick up over-the-counter medicines, baby lotion, soft drinks, or other supplies, you'll find CVS at 200 Biscayne Blvd. (786.838.0316). A few blocks west from Bayfront at 1 SE 3rd Ave. (and E. Flagler St.) is Walgreens (305.373.4320). If you're near Mary Brickell Village, you'll find a good Publix grocery store there (911 SW 1st Avenue, 305.358.1575) approximately 1 block north of the Brickell Metrorail station.

Directly opposite the American Airlines Arena, at 600 Biscayne Boulevard, stands the handsome yellow building Freedom Tower. The 1925 Spanish-inspired landmark was designed by New York firm Schultze and Weaver, which also designed the Coral Gables Biltmore Hotel and the Breakers in Palm Beach. The structure was first home to the *Miami News*. This newspaper began in 1896 as the *Miami Metropolis* and was renamed more than once. (Local Miami figure Bill Baggs was the paper's editor from 1957 to 1969. Besides being a civil rights activist, Baggs campaigned to save acres of Key Biscayne from being turned into yet more condos. Bill Baggs Cape Florida State Park was named in his honor.) The *Miami News* operation eventually moved to the *Miami Herald* building; the paper folded in 1988. In the 1960s the tower became a federal processing center for refugees from the Castro regime. Cuban exiles received medical and dental care here, too. After the government sold it, the tower fell into neglect. Today this beautifully restored structure commemorates the Cuban exiles who have contributed so much to modern Miami. Those with an interest in Cuban history may wish to pop in to see the lobby. The Miami Dade College Gallery displays occasional exhibitions here. An attractive mural shows explorer Ponce de Leon with a Tequesta chief, while galleons and mermaids ride the waves. The lobby hours are 12:00 noon to 5:00 p.m., Tuesday through Friday.

Another historic gem can be found approximately 6 blocks south and a few blocks west: the Olympia Theater at the Gusman Center for the Performing Arts. Constructed in 1926, its Mediterranean Revival architecture has been enchanting theater and music fans for decades. Inside, kids will see charming Moorish decoration, turrets, towers, and balconies, with electric "stars" and man-made "clouds" overhead. Go to the website http://www.gusmancenter.org for the schedule and to purchase tickets. The theater's address is 174 E. Flagler Street and the phone number is 305.374.0303.

One of Downtown's greatest cultural cornerstones is the distinctive glass-and-steel Adrienne Arsht Center for the Performing Arts. The complex includes buildings on both sides of Biscayne Boulevard, designed by Argentine-born architect Cesar Pelli. One of the largest performing arts centers in the United States, it showcases touring theater, music, dance, etc., and is home to the Miami Symphony Orchestra, the Miami City Ballet, the Florida Grand Opera, Broadway Across America, and Jazz Roots. The celebrated Cleveland Orchestra performs a series here, too. Past productions include *Mary Poppins* the musical, the *Nutcracker* ballet, famed classical guitarist Angel Romero with the Miami Symphony Orchestra, Joshua Bell, and the Miami Flamenco Festival. Tickets can be purchased on their website, and parking can also be reserved online. Ticket prices vary significantly, depending on the performance. Check their website for Family Fest days, which are free and designed for kids.

The Adrienne Arsht Center for the Performing Arts
1300 Biscayne Blvd.
Miami 33132
Box office 305.949.6722
http://www.arshtcenter.org
Ages: M, TW, TN

In the midst of the tall contemporary buildings, 3 historic houses of worship—Episcopal, Catholic, and Jewish—have survived the bulldozers of development. Erected in 1925, Trinity Cathedral is the diocesan seat for the Episcopal Church in South Florida. One of the oldest churches in Miami, the cathedral has a soaring exterior and a serene, tropical interior. Architect Harold Hastings Mundy designed the Romanesque Revival exterior, with a cross set in the rose window. The vintage mosaic-tile mural behind the altar makes for a handsome focal point during worship. Sunday Eucharist takes place at 8:00 a.m., 10:00 a.m., and in Spanish at 12:15 p.m. (464 NE 16th Street, http://www.trinitymiami.org). The parish of Gesu Catholic Church was founded in 1896, although the current building, with Italian marble and German stained glass, was erected in the 1920s. Before the 1961 Bay of Pigs invasion of Cuba, thousands of people came here for mass. Mass is held at this lovely pale pink church 7 days a week. On Sundays a bilingual mass is celebrated at 8:30 a.m., mass in Spanish at 10:30 a.m. and 1:00 p.m., and mass in English at 11:30 a.m. (118 NE 2nd Street, http://www.gesuchurch.org).

The main historic sanctuary at Temple Israel of Greater Miami was constructed in 1927 by the same architects who designed the Wolfsonian-FIU Museum building on South Beach; it is now on the National Register of Historic Places. The Gumenick Chapel, built in 1969, features the dramatically stunning architecture of Kenneth Treister. At this progressive, urban temple, Friday evening Shabbat services start around 7:30 p.m., while Saturday morning service runs from 9:30 to 11:00 a.m. (137 NE 19th Street, http://www.templeisrael.net).

Restaurants

In Downtown, Bayside Marketplace contains several informal dining options, some of which are described below. Just south of Downtown lies the Brickell neighborhood and the Mary Brickell Village shopping center (901 S. Miami Avenue), where you'll find ethnic and chain restaurants, including P. F. Chang's, Doraku Sushi, Grimpa Brazilian Steakhouse, Fado Irish Pub, and Rosa Mexicano, in addition to the Burger and Beer Joint described below. Mary Brickell Village is located 1 to 2 blocks from the Metrorail, which also makes stops Downtown.

BURGER AND BEER JOINT

Mary Brickell Village, 901 S. Miami Ave., 305.523.2244, http://www. bnbjoint.com

Tweens and teens may appreciate the rock 'n' roll atmosphere that pervades this hamburger-focused restaurant. Burgers are thick and juicy, often with gourmet toppings. For parents, there is an extensive selection of beers.

$ SPLURGE

EDGE STEAK AND BAR

Four Season Hotel, 1435 Brickell Ave., 305.381.3190, http://www.
edgerestaurant.com

When a special occasion calls for a lavish Sunday brunch, the stylish Edge delivers. While savoring dramatic Downtown views, you can choose among grill-to-order barbecue, crab claws, jumbo shrimp, oysters, paella, suckling pig, whole red snapper, and a mind-blowing selection of desserts. There is a small children's buffet station next to the children's play area; some dishes for kids can be ordered à la carte. Adults $65, children $32 (5–12), children 4 and under free, on Sundays from 11:30 a.m. to 3:00 p.m. Breakfast, lunch, and dinner are also served throughout the week. Reservations can be made online.

LOS RANCHOS STEAKHOUSE

Bayside Marketplace, 401 Biscayne Blvd., 305.375.8188, http://www.
beststeakinmiami.com

This Latin American steakhouse offers a limited children's menu, along with steaks, rich soups, salads, and appetizers.

PERRICONE'S MARKETPLACE AND CAFE

10 SE 10th St. (Brickell), Miami 33131, 305.374.9449, http://www.
perricones.com

This Italian eatery welcomes loyal crowds for lunch, dinner, and their weekend brunch buffets. You'll find Italian classics and other dishes (such as a cashew-encrusted salmon salad) along with a children's menu. Weekend nights and brunch can grow crowded.

TRADEWINDS WATERFRONT BAR AND GRILL

Bayside Marketplace, 401 Biscayne Blvd., 305.416.6944, http://www.
tradewindsbarandgrill.com

With a view over Pier 5, Tradewinds is a classic seafront restaurant that serves oysters Rockefeller, whole fried fish, paella, pizza, and sandwiches. The children's menu includes mini burgers and grilled cheese.

TRULUCK'S

777 Brickell Ave., Miami 33131, 305.579.0035, http://www.trulucks.com

Widely praised Truluck's serves chilled seafood platters for 2 or 4, decadent steaks, and an enticing range of fish, lobster, and crab. Located in the Suntrust Building at 8th Street, this is an elegant, grown-up establishment where you'll take the kids when they've promised to be on best behavior. Entrées average $30 to $50.

Accommodations

Most visitors who stay in Downtown hotels are either there for business, sporting and cultural events, or for a cruise departure. Although there are good quality rooms and facilities to be found, getting in and out of this area by car can be a challenge during the rush-hour commute. Events such as Miami Heat games, the Ultra Music Festival, the Miami Book Fair, and the ING marathon can bring Downtown traffic to a standstill. The Metrorail and the Metromover allow for limited public transportation options, while the new Biscayne-Brickell Trolley buses take passengers on a helpful north-south loop.

CASA MODERNA MIAMI

1100 Biscayne Blvd., Miami 33132, 786.369.0300, http://www.casamodernamiami.com

This upscale high-rise hotel boasts impressive public spaces, sleek baths, well-appointed rooms, and comfortable beds. Discounted room rates for 2 adults and 2 children can go as low as $188, while typical rates can average $314. It's close to the American Airlines Arena and a short drive from Jungle Island and the Miami Children's Museum on Watson Island. The 14th floor Sky Pool and deck look like a photo in a glossy décor magazine, and the Amuse Restaurant serves up breakfast and lunch options that can work for kids (although the well-curated dinner dishes may work best for adult date-nights).

HAMPTON INN DOWNTOWN AND BRICKELL

50 SW 12th St., Miami 33130, 305.377.9400, http://www.hamptoninnmiamibrickell.com

Not all Hampton Inns are created equal, and this well-run, good-looking hotel is certainly one of the chain's nicer representatives, with modern décor, fitness room, rooftop pool, free buffet breakfast, and light-hearted tropical art. Parking costs $18 per day. In summer, a room with 2 queen beds (sleeping 2 adults and 2 children) starts at $189, not including tax.

INTERCONTINENTAL HOTEL

100 Chopin Plaza, Miami 33131, 305.577.1000, http://www.icmiamihotel.com

One convenience of this hotel is that it contains 4 restaurants, including their poolside lunch spot, Blue Water. Rooms and suites are decorated in a contemporary style, and many have bay views. Summer rates for 2 adults and 2 children start at $172, although websites such as http://www.hotwire.com may offer better deals. The 34-story hotel features a workout room and spa services, in addition to its pool. It's convenient to the Metromover, Bayfront Park, and, for cruise passengers, PortMiami.

10

Wynwood and the Design District

Tucked north of Downtown are crowded blocks of warehouses and storefronts that make up the Wynwood Arts District. Art galleries face out onto asphalt streets and concrete sidewalks, bare of vegetation except for languid palm trees. Street murals pop with vivid pigments and shapes. Away from the main roads small houses, often painted in bright colors, are little oases of everyday life, with tropical gardens relieving the industrial expanses of cement.

Historically, Wynwood had a large, working-class Puerto Rican population and was called "Little San Juan." Small Puerto Rican stores and restaurants did (and still do) business in modest buildings. Gradually, the number of Puerto Ricans has decreased as some moved elsewhere in Miami, and Hondurans partially took their place. As the 20th century drew to a close, Wynwood's identity as a blue-collar, ethnic neighborhood and manufacturing zone started to shift.

An art exhibition at the David Castillo Gallery. Photo by Laura Albritton.

In the early 2000s, artists who sought inexpensive studio space began to create in Wynwood. Adventuresome gallery owners opened their doors to exhibit exuberant, local art. Sculptor Pepe Mar remembers, "There was a certain energy in the air; you had emerging artists, working together, showing with the same people over and over again." Shows cropped up in temporary spaces, and collectors soon paid attention to this once-neglected corner of Miami. Yet to venture to Wynwood meant braving a rather tough neighborhood. Mar recalls, "It was a rough area—you would see drug addicts on the street every morning. Now there are cafés and restaurants." Today, Wynwood has gentrified, and the galleries look much more established. Studio space is no longer cheap for up-and-coming young artists, and trendy restaurants and cafes cater to a culturally minded clientele. In fact, its popularity as an entertainment hub has driven rents up; some galleries are decamping to Downtown or elsewhere. That said, Wynwood has not become entirely polished or transformed; the streets still exude a slight roughness.

⊘ SURVIVAL TIP

To reach Wynwood from Downtown or south of Downtown (Coconut Grove, Coral Gables, South Miami), it's better to stick to the highway, I-95, then take its east-bound off-shoot 195. (There are still marginal neighborhoods near Wynwood and Downtown.) Once on 195 heading toward Miami Beach, take the 2A exit for N. Miami Avenue. You'll turn right onto N. Miami Avenue, then right onto 29th Street, and finally, to visit some of the main galleries, turn left onto NW 2nd Avenue and look for street parking.

The art in Wynwood tends toward the cutting edge, experimental, and contemporary. For example, at David Castillo Gallery, Mexican-born sculptor Pepe Mar has exhibited intriguing figures assembled from baskets and found objects, coated them in bright paint and gold leaf; Tina La Porta uses medicinal pills to create striking images and sculpture (Robert Fontaine Gallery). Clemencia Labin's work features pop art colors and incorporates everyday objects, from plastic handbags to bikini fabric (Diana Lowenstein Gallery). Brazilian Jaildo Marinho crafts striking 2- and 3-dimensional work, whose primary colors recall the palette and geometry of Piet Mondrian and Kazimir Malevich (at Durban Segnini Gallery).

♀ INSIDE SCOOP

The second Saturday of every month Wynwood holds an Art Walk (from 7:00 to 10:00 p.m.) when galleries stay open into the evening. Many give out free wine, soft drinks, and even snacks to visitors. Parents can get into the spirit by dressing in black or haute-bohemian attire. What makes it especially child-friendly are the food trucks located at 210 NW 22nd Lane. From 6:00 p.m. to 12:00 midnight around 25 to 40 trucks dish out their specialties, from grilled cheese sandwiches to barbecue to mini burgers. Combining an evening of popping into galleries with some inexpensive comfort food eaten out-of-doors makes this cultural experience more accessible. Keep in mind that later in the evening the streets grow packed with hard-drinking, sometimes rowdy crowds; if you bring children, it's easier to venture out during the first hour of Second Saturday Art Walks. The website http://www.wynwoodartwalk.com has helpful information, a directory of galleries and restaurants, and online tickets for their 1-hour Wynwood tour ($18 per person).

If your family isn't able to make it to Second Saturday Art Walk, you can easily put together your own walking tour of the district. Some galleries are located on the same block, so children don't have to amble very far to see a range of exhibitions. Most galleries lie between NW 20th Street and NW 36th Street, west of North Miami Avenue. If your kids aren't used to galleries or museums, prepare them with the basics: don't touch the art, don't run, don't yell, etc. Because most galleries are small, they can be seen quickly, which helps ward off children's boredom.

Enterprising parents can also turn the art-viewing experience into a game: "Which piece would you pick for your bedroom?" For future collectors: "Guess which piece costs the most money?" (Ask the staff for a price list.) If the gallery allows photography, tweens can post pictures of "Strange Art" to Facebook or Instagram. Some galleries tend to be closed on Mondays, and open Tuesdays through Saturdays from approximately 10:00 a.m. to 5:00 p.m. (although it varies). Once in a while, an exhibition may contain images or features disturbing to children; if there are 2 parents on this outing, 1 can quickly head inside and scope out the art. If you're a single parent, ask staff if the work is child-appropriate. (You may want to spell out what you mean by "child-appropriate," since not everyone holds the same views on this subject.) Entrance to galleries is free, making a visit to Wynwood not only cultural but also budget-friendly.

Some galleries you may wish to visit are:

David Castillo Gallery, 2234 NW 2nd Ave., 305.573.8110
Diana Lowenstein Gallery, 2043 N. Miami Ave., 305.576.1804
Dot Fiftyone Gallery, 51 NW 36th St., 305.573.9994
Durban Segnini Gallery, 2145 NW 2nd Ave., 305.774.7740

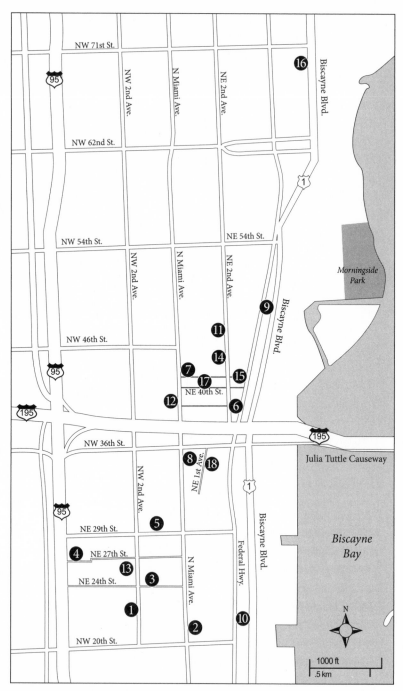

Wynwood and the Design District

Emerson Dorsch Gallery, 151 NW 24th St., 305.576.1278
Gallery Diet, 174 NW 23rd St., 305.571.2288
Gary Nader Fine Art, 62 NE 27th St., 305.576.0256
Locust Projects, 3852 N. Miami Ave., 305.576.8570
Robert Fontaine Gallery, 2349 NW 2nd Ave., 305.397.8530

"Wynwood Walls" is a street-art, mural project conceptualized by the late Tony Goldman, an important developer in South Beach and the arts district. Six dumpy warehouses got creative makeovers as painters brought out their most vivid colors and bold graphics. Each year, the murals are covered over, and new works are created on top. Artists from the United States, Mexico, Japan, Brazil, and Belgium have contributed wild images. Located at 2550 NW 2nd Avenue (at NW 25th Street), Wynwood Walls brings vitality to the area and has inspired artists to paint exterior walls in other sections of the neighborhood.

Two major private collections have opened to the public in Wynwood. The Margulies Collection at the Warehouse is housed in 45,000 square feet of space and features masterpieces of abstract expressionism, pop art, minimalism, and conceptual art. A visit here allows you and your children a chance to see some of the major art developments in the 20th and 21st centuries. Although not all children will find the art thrilling, there's a fairly good chance that some pieces will grab their attention. The exhibitions change, and the Margulies Collection is open only part of the year, from approximately October 17 to April 27; check on the website or call, as these dates may vary from year to year.

Map Key

1. David Castillo Gallery
2. Diana Lowenstein Fine Arts
3. Dorsch Gallery
4. Margulies Collection
5. Rubell Family Collection
6. Jonathan Adler
7. De La Cruz Contemporary Art Space
8. The Shops at Midtown
9. Publix

10. Bacardi Building
11. Buena Vista Deli
12. Harry's Pizzeria
13. Joey's
14. Mandolin Aegean Bistro
15. MC Kitchen
16. Michy's
17. Michael's Genuine Food & Drink
18. Salumeria 104

Margulies Collection at the Warehouse
591 NW 27th St.
Miami 33127
305.576.1051
http://www.margulieswarehouse.com
Adults $10
Wednesday through Saturday 11:00 a.m. to 4:00 p.m. (open only
part year; check website for dates)
Ages: M, TW, TN

The Rubell Family Collection is one of the largest private art collections in the world. Housed in 45,000 square feet, this huge building hosts exhibitions that also travel to other institutions. The collection includes work by famous artists such as Jean-Michel Basquiat, Keith Haring, Damien Hirst, Jeff Koons, Cindy Sherman, Kara Walker, and Andy Warhol. Some exhibitions may intrigue kids; others may contain images that are *extremely* inappropriate for children. Signs posted here warn parents of sections that are distressing or upsetting for young ones. Nevertheless, if you plan to take children, ask staff for concrete advice about where to go—and where to avoid—before venturing in.

The Rubell Family Collection
95 NW 29th St.
Miami 33127
305.573.6090
http://www.rfc.museum
Adults $10, 18 years and under $5
Wednesday through Saturday 10:00 a.m. to 6:00 p.m., closed August
Ages: Depends upon the exhibition. Some artwork here is *not*
child-appropriate.

The Design District

Just north of Wynwood you'll come to Miami's Design District. The Design District contains a small grid of streets lined with shops. Giant plate-glass windows display handsome leather furnishings, bath fixtures, innovative chairs, and fine linens. Design buffs looking for fabulous interior décor, or window shoppers who dream of redecorating will enjoy a stroll through this chic commercial center. Here you'll also find architecture firms, antique stores, and creative enterprises.

Like the Wynwood Arts District, the Design District once appeared rough and neglected, with abandoned or run-down warehouses and commercial buildings. Starting in the late 1990s certain pioneers saw the potential for a new kind of district in the city. Design and art ventures opened, and the area slowly blossomed. Outsiders began snapping up historic homes in the adjacent Buena Vista neighborhood. Gradually, restaurants opened their doors for business. Today the quarter continues to grow larger and more polished. It's an international, artistic oasis. Gay and lesbian parents should find both the Design District and Wynwood two of the more gay-friendly parts of Miami.

The Design District's central grid of streets (with the most density of shops) is not by any means huge. The area's boundaries run from NE 38th Street to NE 42nd Street, between NE 2nd Avenue and N. Miami Avenue, a total of only .2 square miles. Sometimes, despite the high-end stores, it feels fairly quiet. (And at night it's better to park near your destination or valet your car.) One noteworthy sight is the Moore Building at 4040 NE 2nd Avenue. Built in 1921, it's been renovated thanks to owner and Design District mover-and-shaker Craig Robins. In the atrium the theatrical white sculpture "Elastika" by renowned architect Zaha Hadid extends overhead. The Moore Building originally housed a furniture store and was the brainchild of T. V. Moore, Miami's "Pineapple King." (In fact, this urban area was once a pineapple plantation.)

Whether or not the Design District is an ideal destination for you and your kids really depends on how interested you all are in expensive modern chairs, unusual chandeliers, or an amazing

High-end clothing stores have joined furnishing and design boutiques in the Design District. Photo by Zickie Allgrove.

pair of high heels. (Not to mention innovative restaurants with some of the best cuisine in the city.) If these don't sound appealing, a visit to the Design District will probably be a waste of an afternoon.

Some of the notable design stores are:

Abitare, 21 NE 39th St., 305.573.5200
Armani/Casa, 10 NE 39th St., 305.573.4331
JANUS et Cie, 3930 NE 2nd Ave., 305.438.0005
Kartell, 155 NE 40th St., 305.573.4010
Luminaire Lab, 160 NE 40th St., 305.576.4662
Monica James and Co., 140 NE 40th St., 305.576.6222
The Rug Company, 4040 NE 2nd Ave., 305.576.9868

$ SPLURGE

Jonathan Adler's "Happy Chic" aesthetic floods his store, with his delightful signature pottery, accessories, and rugs. Some of his items will appeal to kids and are even made for children, such as a recent "junior elephant" pillow ($38), lion needlepoint pillow ($98), and a giraffe nightlight ($48). Needlepoint pillows, ice buckets, and table lamps may tempt the grown-ups. Jonathan Adler, 4040 NE 2nd Avenue, 305.576.0200.

Recently, fashion boutiques have established outposts here, and now exquisite shoes, tops, and jewelry are elegantly displayed at boutiques such as Marni, Céline, Prada, Cartier, Christian Louboutin, Maison Martin Margiela, and Sebastian James. The emphasis is on luxury and carefully curated showrooms.

Addresses for select shops are:

Cartier, 151 NE 40th St., 305.864.873
Céline, 191 NE 40th St., 305.866.1888
Christian Louboutin, 155 NE 40th St., 305.576.6820
Marni, 3930 NE 2nd Ave., 305.764.3357
Prada, 180 NE 40th St., 305.438.2280

Although Wynwood and the Design District are distinct neighborhoods, they run together, and important art offerings can be found in or on the border of the Design District. During Art Basel Miami Beach in December, a concurrent art fair, Art Miami, is located in northern Wynwood, at the southern boundary of the Design District. Art Miami hosts art dealers from around the world, who display their most interesting paintings, sculptures, and installations for collectors and the viewing public.

✳ DEAL

The Design District is home to one of Miami's major collections. The De La Cruz Collection Contemporary Art Space was launched by Rosa and Carlos de la Cruz and functions as a private museum. With 3 stories and 30,000 square feet, the Contemporary Art Space exhibits dazzling contemporary artworks; the institution also provides support for artists and funds educational initiatives for local schoolchildren. Admission here is free, and exhibitions change every few months. If you have time to take your kids to only 1 institution in the arts districts, this is certainly an excellent place to visit. You can check online for the current exhibition.

De La Cruz Contemporary Art Space
23 NE 41st St.
305.576.6112
http://www.delacruzcollection.org
Free admission
Monday through Saturday 10:00 a.m. to 4:00 p.m., closed Sunday
Ages: M, TW, TN
(Babies and toddlers are welcome, and they may even be interested in the exciting shapes and colors.)

 ## RAINY DAY

Sometimes even the most devoted art and design fans need a pragmatic break—particularly when traveling with children. The Shops at Midtown Miami offer the chance to do budget shopping, pick up supplies or clothing, and sit down for an inexpensive burger. Target anchors this 3-story complex; other stores include Marshalls, Payless, Loehmann's, Party City, and West Elm. Dining options include Five Guys Burgers, Lime Fresh Mexican Grill, Pasta Folies, Giraffas Brazilian Steaks and Burgers, and Yogurbella. Hours for the plaza are 10:00 a.m. to 9:00 p.m., except Sundays (12:00 noon to 6:00 p.m.)

The Shops at Midtown Miami
3401 N. Miami Ave.
Miami 33127
http://www.shopmidtownmiami.com

 ## NECESSITIES

The Target store mentioned above carries a large selection of baby supplies, snacks, over-the-counter medicines, and sunscreen. The Publix grocery store located nearby on Biscayne Boulevard also sells diapers, formula, snacks, and a wide range of groceries. Publix, 4870 Biscayne Blvd., Miami 33137, 305.573.8601.

Close to the Design District are notable examples of MiMo architecture. MiMo, or Miami Modern, evolved from the late 1940s to the mid-1960s, especially in Mid-Beach and on a stretch of Biscayne Boulevard. The most famous proponent of this glamorous, over-the-top style was renowned architect Morris Lapidus, who designed the Fontainebleau Hotel and Lincoln Road on Miami Beach. Architecture buffs may wish to take a short detour from the Design District and go to Biscayne Boulevard to look at some of the remaining whimsical, retro structures. The handsome Bacardi Building (2100 Biscayne) was designed by Enrique Gutierrez. Its gorgeous blue-and-white tile murals were created by Brazilian Francisco Brennand, and the plant motifs recall the Bacardi family's roots in Xiches, Spain. At 2919 Biscayne the TechnoMarine Building's panels have wavy lines that contrast with a strict, modernist grid. Edwin Reeder designed the Shalimar Motel (6200 Biscayne) in 1955, with its U-shape and eaves that slope dramatically downward. The South Pacific Motel (6300 Biscayne) has a bizarrely heavy, faux stone façade at the lobby, which looks more Old West than Polynesian. The Vagabond Motel (7301 Biscayne) boasts a fountain with Amazon-like sea-nymphs and rearing dolphins. At this point you'll be in the "Upper East Side," which is a different neighborhood, close to the award-winning restaurant Michy's (see Restaurants section).

Restaurants

Some of Miami's most innovative, successful restaurants can be found in Wynwood, the Design District, neighboring Buena Vista, and the Upper East Side. Many tend to be focused on adults, rather than kids. This doesn't mean you can't take your children. (Miami parents certainly do!) Sometimes you might need to be creative, though, and let children split dishes or have a child share with you.

Locals love the Buena Vista Deli for its French pastries, sandwiches, salads, and quiches. Photo by Zickie Allgrove.

BUENA VISTA DELI

4590 NE 2nd Ave., Miami 33137 (Buena Vista/Design District),
305.576.3945, http://www.buenavistadeli.com

Buena Vista Deli offers delectable French pastries, sandwiches, and other tasty plates for amazingly good prices. Serving breakfast, lunch, and dinner, this is a child-friendly and easy option with outside seating and some indoor tables facing their bakery case.

BUENA VISTA BISTRO

4582 NE 2nd Ave., Miami 33137 (Buena Vista/Design District),
305.456.5909, http://www.buenavistabistro.com

Owned by the same folks as the deli, the bistro serves more substantial meals in a dining room, from escargot to salmon to curry chicken. Open for lunch and dinner, this small locale is the laid-back creation of a French chef.

HARRY'S PIZZERIA

3918 N. Miami Ave., Miami 33137 (Design District), 786.275.4963,
http://www.harryspizzeria.com

The chef of Michael's (see below) started this more casual place that serves pizza from wood-burning ovens made with only the finest ingredients. Desserts are a standout. This informal hangout has daily dinner specials and craft beers.

JOEY'S

2506 NW 2nd Ave., Miami 33127 (Wynwood), 305.438.0488, http://www.joeyswynwood.com

Joey's is a stylish but relaxed Italian restaurant with an open kitchen. Gnocchi, lamb chops, polenta, and baked cod keep customers returning again and again. The dining room feels modern, stylish, and unstuffy.

MANDOLIN AEGEAN BISTRO

4312 NE 2nd Ave., Miami 33137 (Design District), 305.576.6066, http://www.mandolinmiami.com

This charming small restaurant, with outdoor and indoor seating, cooks Greek and Turkish food. Their small garden underlines the emphasis placed on fresh ingredients, in dishes such as the roasted peppers with feta and a sirloin and lamb cheeseburger.

MC KITCHEN

4141 NE 2nd Ave., Miami 33137 (Design District), 305.456.9948, http://www.mckitchenmiami.com

Antipasti such as halibut crudo and roasted head-on langoustines let you know MC Kitchen isn't your ordinary Italian *ristorante*. Dinner translates to beautifully done fish and delicate pasta; due to its popularity, reservations are recommended for dinner.

MICHY'S

6927 Biscayne Blvd., Miami 33138 (Upper East Side), 305.759.2001, http://www.michysmiami.com

Headed by well-known chef and James Beard winner Michelle Bernstein, this trendy bistro has fabulous Miami décor and serves up scrumptious items like white gazpacho, creamy polenta with truffle-poached egg, and seared flounder. A great place for foodies, Michy's is open only for dinner. It's in the Upper East Side, an area close to—but definitely not in—the Design District. Reservations recommended.

MICHAEL'S GENUINE FOOD AND DRINK

130 NE 40th St., Miami 33137 (Design District), 305.573.5550, http://www.michaelsgenuine.com

One of Miami's best-regarded restaurants is run by chef and James Beard winner Michael Schwartz. He and his crew aren't kidding around about fresh ingredients. Dishes range from small to extra-large plates, making this a great place to try new things. From sweet and spicy pork belly to chargrilled octopus, the food has won many raves.

SALUMERIA 104

3451 NE 1st Ave., #104, Miami 33137 (Wynwood), 305.424.9588, http://www.salumeria104.com

This salami shop and trattoria specializes in gorgeous-tasting prosciutto. Home-made pasta and a variety of dishes, from pork chops to quail, set Salumeria 104 apart from the mundane. Best for kids who are willing to be adventuresome.

Accommodations

Despite their popularity, the Design District and Wynwood do not yet offer much in the way of accommodations. Certain local motels have struggled in the past—and for that reason are not recommended here. If you wish to stay as close as possible, your best bet lies either in Downtown or on Miami Beach. Mid-Beach is only a short ride over the Julia Tuttle Causeway (I-195) while South Beach, although a bit further, is still quite accessible.

Further Afield

For families who have time to explore further afield, Miami serves as an excellent gateway to 2 incredibly beautiful parts of Florida: the Everglades and the Keys. Day-trips are completely do-able, while those who wish to discover these extraordinary landscapes in greater depth can easily fill a weekend or longer. Viewed from a distance, the Everglades can appear to be just miles and miles of reedy swamp. Yet these wetlands actually form a river—in the rainy season—that flows from Lake Okeechobee down to the southern tip of Florida. Stretching around 60 miles wide, the water moves at an unhurried rate, so that a single drop can spend years on its journey to empty into Florida Bay. This massive area, about 100 miles long, is vital for southern Florida's ecology, water quality, and flood control.

The Everglades' treasures and secrets necessitate close-up exploration. You can encourage children to notice the birds that hunt, nest, and hide among the grasses and trees: ibises with their curved scarlet beaks, elegant white and blue herons, egrets poking through tall grasses, or a rare Wood Stork with its wings fringed in black. Near seawater, pelicans soar overhead in

Pelicans wobble when they walk but become supremely graceful as they take to the sky. Their pouches expand to catch fish. Courtesy of the U.S. National Park Service. Photo by Rodney Cammauf.

graceful formation. Lucky visitors might spot a Roseate Spoonbill, the pinkish birds with the uncommonly rounded bill, or a small white-tailed Keys deer. Extremely fortunate folks will glimpse an endangered Florida panther. The most famous resident is, of course, the alligator, surveying the world with beady eyes as the rest of its powerful body remains submerged in the murky water.

The Everglades was once home to early Indian tribes, the Calusa and later the Tequesta (who did not survive European settlement). During the Seminole Indian Wars in the 1800s, when American settlers pressured the U.S. government to remove tribal peoples from the Florida peninsula, some Seminole and Miccosukee took refuge in the Everglades. Today, in addition to its national parks, the "River of Grass" is also home to Indian reservations.

For visitors with only a short amount of time, the Everglades Alligator Farm gives you a brief introduction to the splendor of this natural world, along with some high-energy fun. This well-run attraction is located in Homestead about 5 miles from the Florida Turnpike. Their airboat rides, which depart 25 minutes after the hour, take you out into the wild. Airboats are essentially vessels propelled by enormous fans and zip along the top of the water. They also tend to be very loud, so forewarn your kids. Airboats can get going quite fast, a tremendously fun activity for most children (but probably too intense for babies or toddlers.) Your guide will slow down to point out flora and fauna and try to ensure you see an alligator in its natural habitat.

Back at the farm, make sure you attend the alligator wrestling show (11:00 a.m., 2:00 p.m., 5:00 p.m.). Alligator wrestling was a technique devised by tribal peoples to capture and defend themselves from alligators. These reptiles, with brains the size of a pea, cannot be tamed, and grappling with any adult alligator is indeed dangerous. Kids will learn about alligator biology and habits. At the end of the show, they get the chance to hold a baby alligator.

The Snake Show teaches the audience about various types of snakes, particularly those found in the Everglades. Children can handle a large snake at the close of the show (10:00 a.m., 1:00 p.m., 4:00 p.m.). The Alligator Feeding session is not for the faint-hearted, as these hungry monsters lunge and snap for food; it's sure to be one of the memorable sights of your vacation (12:00 p.m., 3:00 p.m.). All in all, the Everglades Alligator Farm does a good job of combining entertainment with educational information. Discount coupons are at times posted on their website; you will need to print these out in advance.

Everglades Alligator Farm
40351 SW 192nd Ave.
Homestead 33034
305.247.2628
http://www.everglades.com
Adults $23 (shows and airboat ride), children 4–11 $15.50 (shows and airboat ride), $15.50 and $10.50 admission (for shows only)
9:00 a.m. to 6:00 p.m., 7 days a week
Ages: B/T, M, TW, TN

If you head north from the attraction on 192nd Avenue and drive approximately 3.8 miles, you'll come to Robert Is Here, a fruit stand that makes spectacularly good milk shakes from all sorts of exotic fruit. Fans of key lime pie will savor the tart key lime shake, which costs $5 plus tax. The store sells fruit,

Visitors to the Everglades Alligator Farm or the Keys stop off at Robert Is Here for fruit shakes and fresh produce. Photo by Zickie Allgrove.

vegetables, flowers, honey, jams, and fresh juices; in the back is an animal pen with goats, emus, donkeys, chickens, and geese. Their new Splash Park is a small water feature where children can cool off. Live music is performed on weekends. Robert Is Here is a popular, "old-time Florida" stop for adults and children alike.

Robert Is Here Fruit Stand and Farm
19200 SW 344th St.
Homestead 33034
305.246.1592
http://www.robertishere.com
8:00 a.m. to 7:00 p.m., 7 days a week
Closed September and October

If your family has more time for the Everglades, you can venture further into this natural sanctuary and spend a night or more. You will have time to explore the vast, wide planes of swamplands, sawgrass lands, coastal prairies, and mangrove forests. Manatees, alligators, fish, birds, and other small wildlife thrive in this protected region; as you and your children move into their habitat, you'll begin to appreciate the incredible beauty. For those adventurous travelers who want a firsthand experience, in the Everglades National Park there are campsites available for $16 per night, in addition to the $10 park entrance (per vehicle). You will need to bring your own camping equipment and make a campsite reservation in advance. The Flamingo Campground has solar-heated showers, bathrooms, picnic tables, and grills. There are nature trails, boating, and winter ranger programs.

⃠ SURVIVAL TIP

Be aware that camping here in the hot, humid, and mosquito-laden months of June, July, August, and September can be downright unpleasant; the temperatures remain relatively high at night, so there isn't much relief from the heat. Rain makes a frequent appearance between June and the end of October. If you're determined to camp this time of year, check the weather frequently and ensure your tent is waterproof.

In the dry winter months, however, spending a night in the midst of the Everglades, with layers of stars overhead, far from the clamor and clatter of cities, can be an unforgettable experience. The U.S. National Park Service website has a plentitude of options and information including a video about how to plan your visit.

To reach the Flamingo Campground from Miami, drive south on the Florida Turnpike until it ends and merges with U.S. 1 in Florida City. At the first traffic light, turn right onto Palm Drive and look for signs to the park. From the main entrance (the Ernest Coe Visitor Center) you'll then continue on for another 38 miles until you reach Flamingo. If using a GPS, use the GPS coordinates rather than the name (GPS 25°08'28.96" N 80°55'25.73" W). If camping, pack food to cook, drinks, mosquito repellant, charcoal, necessities for kids and babies, and any other camping supplies. The gift shop at the privately run Flamingo Marina does sell some snacks, sandwiches, basic groceries, soft drinks, beer, and wine—but the selection is limited and it closes at 7:00 p.m.

To make the most of your time in the Everglades, rent canoes, kayaks, or a fishing skiff at the Flamingo Marina. The advantage of taking a small vessel out into the water is the opportunity it affords your family to see birds, wildlife, and plant life close up, without the noise of an airboat. (Real fans of kayaking who intend on spending ample time in the Everglades may want to purchase *A Paddler's Guide to Everglades National Park* by Johnny Molloy.) The Flamingo Marina staff will give you a map and show you where to paddle. If you'd rather have someone else do the navigating, take the guided Florida Bay tour, which costs $30 per adult, $15 for children (5–12), and is free for children 5 and under. Rates, details, and online reservation forms are available at the marina website, which is different from the National Park website: http://www.evergladesnationalparkboattoursflamingo. com. Or you can call the Flamingo Marina at 239.695.3101.

Flamingo Visitor Center
GPS 25°08'28.96" N 80°55'25.73" W
Everglades National Park
9:00 a.m. to 4:30 p.m.
239.695.2945
http://www.nps.gov/ever/
Ages: B/T, M, TW, TN

Some visitors find camping overly rustic—or can't bring all that gear on their trip. In that case, you can still have a close encounter with the Everglades by renting a cabin in Everglades City. One good option is at Miller's World, a privately run, 1-stop shop with restaurant, cabins, marina, and boat rentals. You will need to drive from Miami on the Tamiami Trail westward approximately 80 miles; it's a 2-lane highway with pretty views into the Everglades. At County Road 29, turn left, drive 3 miles, then take a right on Begonia. Continue onto Copeland Avenue, and then take a left onto South Copeland Avenue. At Miller's World there are duplex cabins, private cabins, and stilt houses for rent; the low season rate for a duplex cabin starts at $109 per night, while a stilt house that sleeps 6 is $235 in the high season (not including taxes and fees).

Miller's World also offers the convenience of the Oyster House Restaurant as well as a deli/store for provisions. The Oyster House Restaurant serves seafood and hamburgers and has a children's menu. At the Glades Haven Marina (239.695.2628) you can rent kayaks, canoes, or skiffs to go out into the Everglades; staff here will give you maps and directions to explore part of the Ten Thousand Islands. The main allure of this part of the Everglades is the small, isolated islands where you and your children can explore, shell, and savor alone time.

The marina can also rent you gear to take advantage of the tremendous fishing. Kayaking through the mangroves gives you the opportunity to view sea life and wildlife in a tranquil, close-up setting. Children too young to paddle canoes or kayaks may enjoy the ride through the water more with a camera to capture the sights. Be sure to follow the staff's advice about where to go, and follow the mile markers so you don't get lost.

The website http://www.florida-everglades.com/evercty/ lists a number of tour operators who can guide you and your kids into the wild including fishing guides. In addition to the water activities, there are places to bike and nature trails for hiking. Bike rentals run $20 for half a day. Visitors do bring babies and toddlers here; with a small baby you can, for example, "wear" your child in a baby pack and go hiking. However, some activities such as kayaking and canoeing may be too challenging with very small children. Also, be sure to bring formula, diapers, and other baby gear with you.

Glades Haven Resort at Miller's World
875 S. Copeland Ave.
Everglades City 34139
239.695.2082
http://www.theevergladesflorida.com
Ages: B/T, M, TW, TN

For a serious step back into vintage Florida, stay at the Everglades Rod and Gun Club, also in Everglades City. Its old-time

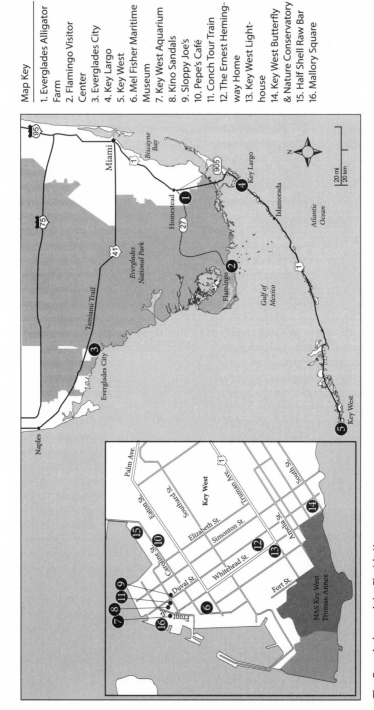

Map Key

1. Everglades Alligator Farm
2. Flamingo Visitor Center
3. Everglades City
4. Key Largo
5. Key West
6. Mel Fisher Maritime Museum
7. Key West Aquarium
8. Kino Sandals
9. Sloppy Joe's
10. Pepe's Café
11. Conch Tour Train
12. The Ernest Hemingway Home
13. Key West Lighthouse
14. Key West Butterfly & Nature Conservatory
15. Half Shell Raw Bar
16. Mallory Square

The Everglades and the Florida Keys

cottages and wide porch with wicker chairs make this lodge a homey base within this small, historic town. Their restaurant serves seafood, pasta, and sandwiches for lunch and dinner, or they will cook your catch (the fish you've caught). There's a pool and a dock where you can rent skiffs, canoes, or arrange for a guided boat or fishing tour. In-season cottage rooms run $110 to $140, and off-season rooms start at $95. To get there from Miami, follow the directions going to Miller's World, but from Copeland Avenue: at the traffic circle, take the first exit to Broadway Avenue West, which will dead end into Riverside Drive.

Everglades Rod and Gun Club
200 Riverside Dr.
Everglades City 34139
239.695.2101
http://www.evergladesrodandgunclub.com

Other Everglades City dining includes:

CAMELLIA STREET GRILL

    202 Camellia St., 239.695.2003

This fun, laid-back restaurant cooks up pulled pork sandwiches, mussels, and key lime pie by the water.

CITY SEAFOOD

    702 Begonia St., 239.695.4700, http://www.cityseafood1.com

A waterfront, picnic-table kind of place, City Seafood offers a fabulous seafood buffet on Fridays. October through May there are stone crab claws; they also serve breakfast and for lunch grouper sandwiches, shrimp baskets, and even alligator!

Key Largo and Key West

The Keys are an archipelago of islands that lie off the Florida peninsula like small, green quartz stones scattered across a swath of glistening aqua silk. Palms, leafy bougainvillea with hot pink blossoms, and reddish gumbo limbo trees dot the landscape as you drive down the Overseas Highway the 98 miles from Key Largo to Key West. The islands, or "keys" (from the Spanish *cayos*) were formed thousands of years ago out of coral reef, not sand, which accounts for the fact that there are few beaches, and the ones that exist tend to be small. Bridges linking the islands pass over ocean so clear you can see right to the bottom. Seafood joints overlooking the aquamarine water serve up grilled hogfish, seared scallops, and Florida lobster. Vibrant, slow-fading sunsets, viewed from the bayside of the Overseas Highway, are an event at restaurants and bars. Sport fishing, kayaking, boating, swimming, scuba diving, and snorkeling engage visitors with the natural world.

The Keys remain proudly unconventional. The conch is the local mascot. This pink-lipped shell appears on the Conch Republic's flag (created when the Keys temporarily seceded from the United States in 1982). In fact, the nickname for Keys residents, especially Key Westers, is "conchs" (pronounced *conks*). Another peculiarity: Overseas Highway addresses are often given by Mile Marker or "MM," either bayside, abbreviated B/S, or oceanside, abbreviated O/S. In the 1970s Jimmy Buffett moved to Key West and was hugely influenced by the off-beat folks and culture of the town; it's where he put together his famous Coral Reefer Band. Today, songs like "Margaritaville," "Changes in Lattitudes," and "Cheeseburger in Paradise" comprise a kind of official soundtrack for the Florida Keys.

The Keys' mellow vibe contrasts with Miami's urban electricity. From central Miami or Coral Gables it takes only about an hour to reach Key Largo, not counting prime times of rush hour or holiday weekends. The real draw of coming here are the marvels that await underneath the ocean. To see them you'll need to go miles from land by boat, to the coral reefs. Small, Bluehead wrasses appear hardly larger than an adult's palm, while black-and-white striped Sergeant major fish, with their yellow-tinted backs, grow to around 6 inches each. Colorful Yellowtail snapper, Red grouper, and Bermuda blue angelfish dart between undulating sea fans. It's completely absorbing—a rarity in our modern world of electronic distractions.

Key Largo, the northernmost and largest key, is home to John Pennekamp Coral Reef State Park, a base from which snorkeling and scuba charters depart daily. (Charters also depart from private marinas.) Pennekamp is listed on the National Register of Historic Places and has access to the Florida Reef, the third largest in the world. You can certainly make an outing to Pennekamp Park a day-trip from Miami, although others prefer to camp here or to stay at a local hotel.

Teenagers and parents who already have dive certifications can take advantage of the 2-stop, 2-tank dive tours that leave the park twice daily (9:00 a.m. and 1:30 p.m.). These excursions cost $55 per person, not including gear rental ($29). Contact the Pennekamp Dive Shop at 305.451.6322 or click on their page at http://www.pennekamppark.com.

💰 SPLURGE

Pennekamp Dive Shop also offers scuba instruction. The Day Resort Course lasts 1 day and includes 2 instructor-guided dives for $185. PADI Open Water Certification lasts for 3 to 4 days ($485). The price includes equipment.

For most travelers wanting to day-trip from Miami, however, snorkeling is going to be a more manageable proposition. If your children can swim well and are willing to put on a snorkel, mask, and fins, they will see a host of amazingly colorful creatures flash beneath the surface: Rainbow parrotfish, Yellow tangs, and turquoise angelfish. Many snorkeling charters stop at the Key Largo Dry Rocks, where the statue "Christ of the Deep" overlooks the undersea world, amid groove and spur coral formation. Spotted eagle rays and Southern stingrays silently flap through the water while bright tropical fish nose the bottom for a snack.

Charter boats provide snorkeling equipment for a $9 charge, so all you need to bring is sunscreen, towel, drinking water, and snacks. (Wear bathing suits, of course!) Both children and adults will be provided with safety vests, which they are required to wear. These vests can be worn deflated (without air) or inflated, so they act as life jackets. Snorkel charter captains will require that all snorkelers wear the safety vests, inflated or deflated. This guidebook strongly recommends that all children wear *inflated* safety vests on snorkeling trips. (It only takes a few breaths to inflate them.) In winter months you can also rent wetsuits.

The snorkeling charter staff will show you how to snorkel, which is not difficult once you get the hang of breathing through a tube. It's important to find a well-fitting mask for everyone, because leaks can put a serious damper on your viewing experience. After that, you and your kids basically need to float and peer through the sea, with occasional kicks propelling you for a better look at an interesting sea creature. Snorkeling trips go to reefs that can be comfortably seen from the water's surface, unlike some scuba charters. Be sure to caution your children not to touch the reef with their hands or let their fins bump the corals; this literally kills the coral. Damaged and dying reefs are a serious problem in the Keys and throughout the world.

How young is too young to snorkel? When venturing out in waters 15 to 20 feet deep, strong swimmers aged 8 and up may feel comfortable with this activity when wearing an inflated safety vest to keep them afloat. It truly depends on your children's individual level of experience and comfort in the sea. Keep in mind you will need to supervise your kids at every moment and snorkel next to them. Water and wind conditions play a major role in how easy or difficult it will be for kids to snorkel out in open ocean; check with the charter company on current conditions. If there are swells, waves, or strong currents, it becomes more challenging. If you have any doubt about your child's ability to breathe comfortably through a snorkel, try snorkeling off the Pennekamp beach and see how he or she does.

Snorkeling boats leave at 9:00 a.m., 12:00 p.m., 1:45 p.m., and 3:00 p.m. (weather permitting) and cost $29.95 for adults and $24.95 for children, not including equipment. If you wish to make reservations online, you need to do so 3 days in advance at http://www.pennekamppark.com. Even with your online reservation, you will need to purchase your tickets in person 1 hour before the trip. If you are *not* able to make reservations 3 days in advance, call 305.451.6300 to reserve by phone. For snorkeling guidance and terrific history about local wrecks, get a copy of *Snorkeling the Florida Keys* by snorkeling expert and Keys resident Brad Bertelli.

⊘ SURVIVAL TIP

When you reach the reef, the boat could bob up and down in the swells—even if the waves average a mere 1 foot. This motion may not be a problem when your family's swimming and snorkeling, but while taking a break on deck, it's not uncommon for certain passengers to feel seasick. Unfortunately, it's hard to predict who will fall victim to this unpleasant sensation. Pressure point wristbands are often successful at alleviating seasickness (but are most effective if worn before you even leave the dock). If your vacation plans include multiple boating trips, a few pairs of these can come in handy. Children's versions can be ordered online at http://www.kalyx.com or http://www.sears.com. Staying in the water (but not losing track of the boat!) can also combat seasickness.

When children are too young to snorkel, or are not strong swimmers, you can take a glass-bottom boat trip from Pennekamp. The 65-foot *Spirit of Pennekamp* leaves 3 times a day (9:15 a.m., 12:15 p.m., and 3:15 p.m.) for 2-and-a-half-hour tours, weather permitting. You will visit shallow reefs to see colorful corals, barracuda, stingrays, and other gorgeous multicolored fish. You can make reservations online at http://www.pennekamppark.com or call 305.451.6300. The cost is $24 for adults and $17 for children under 12.

If you are not interested in going out on the reefs, Pennekamp does have 2 small man-made beaches. Cannon Beach features a snorkeling spot 100 feet offshore, where the remnants of a Spanish wreck, including sunken cannon, have been arranged. While you won't see the tropical species on a reef, there are small fish to give your kids a taste of snorkeling. This is also a convenient

Children look-
ing at the reef
from the *Spirit
of Pennekamp*,
a glass-bottom
boat. Courtesy
of Florida Keys
News Bureau.
Photo by Bob
Krist.

place to practice with snorkeling equipment. Far Beach is another modest beach with palm trees. On the road just prior to
Far Beach is a children's playground. Keep in mind that these
beaches, like most in the Keys, are petite. Tourists who travel to
Key Largo imagining large stretches of sand and terrific, shallow water for swimming are often disappointed. Seagrasses off
Pennekamp beaches don't attract colorful tropical fish the way
reefs do; also, while the water itself is clear, the dark seagrasses
along the bottom make it more difficult to spot what fish there
are. You'll need to venture out on a boat to take advantage of the
area's true beauty.

The park's Visitor Center is definitely worth stopping by, to check out their large aquarium, tropical fish tanks, and nature videos. Their film about fish found on the reef is a helpful primer for people considering a snorkeling trip. Inside the Concession Building's gift shop you'll find a range of souvenirs; toward the back is also a place to make rental and trip reservations, along with a snack bar with some family-friendly lunch options.

Kayaks and canoes can be rented to explore the channels among the mangroves and the birds and fish. Single kayaks cost $12 an hour, while doubles are $17. Canoes are $20 an hour. Both are available from 8:00 a.m. to 3:45 p.m. (305.451.6300). Powerboats can also be rented; rates for a 20-footer start at $160 for 4 hours (305.451.6325).

If you rent a boat, be sure not to anchor on the reef. (From the surface a reef can look like ordinary rocks!) Every anchor that goes down into the coral does permanent damage. The top layer of coral is alive: tiny, living organisms slowly build the reef, a fraction of an inch each year. Mooring buoys, which are white with a blue stripe, are free for you to use and allow you to tie up with no impact on the environment. Keep in mind that regulations protecting the reefs are vigorously enforced.

In terms of on-land exploration, Pennekamp Park contains 3 fairly short trails. The most scenic is the Mangrove Trail, which takes you on a wooden deck through a mangrove forest and along the water. Signage helps children learn to identify red, black, and white mangroves.

Pennekemp has campsites for tents, along with hot showers and restrooms; the cost is $36 per night. There are grills for cooking, but ground fires are not allowed. To reserve a campsite go to http://www.reserveamerica.com and look up Pennekamp State Park. You will need to bring your own tent and camping equipment. Camping in the Keys in summer, September, and even October and May is not for the faint-hearted. Expect mosquitos, heat, humidity, and rain. Separate from the camping area, the park has additional restroom facilities at Far Beach, the Main Concession building, and the Dive Shop.

~~~~~~

John Pennekamp Coral Reef State Park
102601 Overseas Highway
MM 102.6, O/S
Key Largo 33037
305.451.6300
http://www.pennekamppark.com
$8 park admission per vehicle
8:00 a.m. to sunset
Ages: B/T, M, TW, TN

~~~~~~

Snorkeling and diving outfits crop up practically every few yards in the Key Largo area. If you don't want to pay park admission to Pennekamp, you can still venture out on a variety of vessels, including the *Sundiver III*. The crew at Sundiver Snorkel Tours frequently works with families and their 46-foot boat has plenty of masks, snorkels, fins, and life jackets sized for children. Their Sundiver Station store (with some tempting gear and clothes) is located at about MM 103, B/S (102840 Overseas Highway). Pay for your trip at the store; then they will give you a map and directions to their dock on Ocean Drive (near MM 100, O/S) within the Key West Inn parking lot. Weather permitting, trips leave at 9:00 a.m., 12:00 noon, and 3:00 p.m. Check their website for an internet coupon, which saves about $3 per person. (1.800.654.7369, http://www.snorkelingisfun.com)

⚌ NECESSITIES

To purchase groceries, charcoal, drinks, or other supplies for your stay in Key Largo, you can drive to the Publix Super Market at Tradewinds Plaza, about half a mile from the park entrance. The store is located at MM 101.5, O/S or 101437 Overseas Highway, and their main number is 305.451.0808. The store sells limited baby supplies, such as diapers and formula, and also contains a pharmacy (305.451.5338). Hours are 7:00 a.m. to 10:00 p.m., 7 days a week, although pharmacy hours are shorter (9:00 a.m. to 9:00 p.m. weekdays, 9:00 a.m. to 7:00 p.m. Saturday, and 9:00 a.m. to 5:00 p.m. Sunday).

If you'd like something to remember your trip, the Shell World located at 97600 Overseas Highway in the median of the road (not far south from Mrs. Mac's Kitchen) is arguably the best souvenir shop in the Upper Keys. Yes, there are all kinds of dinky plastic and wooden trinkets you may later regret buying, but the shop also sells eye-catching resort wear, flip-flops, jewelry, books, artwork, toys, and chic home décor items.

RAINY DAY

Situated in a shopping center at MM 91, B/S or 91298 Overseas Highway, Tavernier Towne Cinemas is the only movie theater in the Upper Keys. Look online for film listings or call 305.853.7004. Another destination when avoiding a storm is the giant World Wide Sportsman store in Islamorada at MM 81.5 or 81576 Overseas Highway (305.664.4615). Here you'll find enough fishing gear to outfit a small town. There is also an art gallery, the Zane Grey Lounge, an Everglades aquarium, and the sister ship to Hemingway's beloved boat *Pilar*.

Restaurants

LAZY DAYS

> 79867 Overseas Highway, Islamorada 33036, 305.664.5256, http://www.keysdining.com

A lot of Upper Keys spots seem to cook very similar, standard meals but oceanfront Lazy Days is a cut above. Chef Lupe Ledesma's well-regarded restaurant serves jumbo shrimp in mango chutney, jalapeño-encrusted yellowtail, and middle-neck clams with wine sauce. There are vegetarian pastas and children's dishes, too. Dinner entrées run from about $15.99 to $33.99. The only catch: it's a long drive from John Pennekamp Coral Reef State Park.

The original Mrs. Mac's restaurant remains a Key Largo favorite.
Photo by Zickie Allgrove.

MRS. MAC'S KITCHEN

99336 Overseas Highway, MM 99.4, Key Largo, 305.451.3722, http://
www.mrsmacskitchen.com

Beloved by locals and visitors alike for its kitschy décor and relaxed dinerlike atmosphere, Mrs. Mac's delivers great-tasting
food—including delicious entrées—at prices that are very good
for the Keys. Breakfast, lunch, and dinner. Their newer location—large but without the rustic charm—can be found in the
median slightly further south at MM 99.

PILOT HOUSE

13 Seagate Blvd., MM 99.5, Key Largo 33037, 305.451.3142, http://www.
pilothousemarina.com

This marina-front restaurant on the oceanside can be slightly
hard to find: from John Pennekamp, drive south 3 miles, turn
left on Atlantic Avenue, take the first right on Homestead Avenue, a slight left onto Ocean Bay Drive, and then left onto
Seagate Boulevard. The menu ranges from fried seafood baskets
to expensive fish dishes and a kid's menu. They also feature a

"glass bottom" bar and free food to feed the fish. Wednesday through Saturday live music.

SUNDOWNER'S

103900 Overseas Highway, Key Largo 33037, 305.451.4502, http://www.sundownerskeylargo.com

A great place to watch the sunset (on the bayside of Overseas Highway), Sundowner's has a wide selection of seafood, steaks, sandwiches, salads, and large wine list, along with a kid's menu. An added plus: children can buy fish food to feed the tarpon.

TOWER OF PIZZA

100600 Overseas Highway (B/S), Key Largo 33037, 305.664.8216, http://www.towerofpizzakeylargo.com

Visible from the road due to its large Tower of Pizza sign, this restaurant serves a range of reasonably priced pizzas on home-made dough, along with pasta dishes. A 16-inch large cheese pizza costs $16; a child's spaghetti with tomato sauce is $4.50. Delivery and takeout, too.

Accommodations

HAMPTON INN AT MANATEE BAY

102400 Overseas Highway (B/S), Key Largo 33037, 305.451.3953, http://www.hamptoninnkeylargo.com

For those who want to overnight in Key Largo but prefer not to camp, the Hampton Inn is only about 500 yards from Pennekamp Park. This pleasant, well-run 2-story hotel has a small beach, a pool (heated in winter), a workout room, free buffet breakfast, free Wi-Fi, and free parking. The tiki bar sells drinks at sunset, and there's an entertaining parrot named Mango. Rooms have refrigerator, microwave, and extra sink. The hotel does not contain a restaurant, but there are a number of restaurants nearby. In January, a room for 2 adults and 2 children runs about $239 (found on http://www.expedia.com), while the same room in June costs $199.

ATLANTIC BAY RESORT

160 Sterling Rd., MM 92.5 (B/S), Tavernier 33070, 305.852.5248

If you're not looking for luxury, but need the convenience of a kitchen/living area, Atlantic Bay Resort has efficiencies and a few cottages that constitute a bargain for the expensive Florida Keys. Located in Tavernier at MM 92.5 (about 20 miles south of Pennekamp), this compound consists of cottages, efficiencies, a saline pool, small beach, free Wi-Fi, and grills. Rates for the cheapest efficiency are $109 low season, $175 high season (based on double occupancy; children under 18 are an additional $10 each per night).

Key West

Fans of pastel Bahamian architecture, Ernest Hemingway, and bohemian good times will want to venture down the island chain to the most famous key of them all, Key West. Long before Miami even existed on a map, Key West grew to a thriving town of shipyards, fishing boats, garrisons, and cigar factories. Only 90 miles from Havana, Key West (or *Cayo Hueso*) originally belonged to the Spanish, then the English, and finally in 1822, it became property of the United States. Wrecking, salt farming, and fishing expanded the economy and turned Key West into one of early Florida's most successful cities. As settlers arrived from the northern and southern states and the Bahamas, the buildings developed a particular, hybrid style, with pastel clapboard siding, fanciful gingerbread trim, and welcoming porches, built up from the ground to avoid flood waters and to ventilate the buildings.

The southern-most settlement in the United States, Key West became important strategically, with a naval air station. President Truman established a "winter White House" here. Its remoteness, natural beauty, and bars attracted a literary and artistic following from the 1920s onward; the island continues to be a haven for creative types who find the laissez-faire attitude appealing. Today the main thoroughfare Duval Street is tourist central. Many of the oddball or eccentric saloons and stores have

One of the performers at Mallory Square before sunset. Some of the visitors will return to the cruise ship in the background. The lucky ones will overnight in Key West. Courtesy of Florida Keys News Bureau. Photo by Bob Krist.

been replaced by T-shirt shops, Starbucks, and Banana Republic. Mallory Square, the plaza that toward dusk becomes crowded with vendors, street performers, and visitors awaiting sunset, is partially blocked at times by huge visiting cruise ships. Nevertheless, as you wander through "Old Town's" quaintly named streets among charming houses, where rogue chickens cluck and scratch, and flowering vines decorate white picket fences, it's possible to imagine how it felt to stroll here 100 years ago.

To describe Key West adequately would take an entire guidebook. Visitors often spend anywhere from a long weekend to a week on this unique island. If you take your kids on a day-trip, you'll only have time to get a taste—which will inevitably make you want to return. The drive down the chain of Keys from Miami is a splendid one (except for occasional traffic) with stunning ocean views as you cross more than 30 separate islands, each with its own distinct personality. Once you reach Old Town in Key West, however, you won't need a car. Some vacationers therefore prefer to leave the car behind and let someone else do the driving. One company, Half Price Tour Tickets, has buses that depart Miami Beach at 6:30 a.m. and then leave Key West at 5:45 p.m. for arrival back in Miami at about 10:00 p.m. They offer pickup at many South Beach and Brickell hotels. Round-trip costs $69 (sometimes on sale for $49) and the ride each way lasts approximately 4 hours, with a half-hour stop. You can make reservations on their website at http://www.halfpricetourtickets.com or call 305.444.0707.

The bus will drop you and your family at the Mel Fisher Maritime Museum, which is a kid-friendly place to start your adventure. Mel Fisher was a visionary treasure hunter who spent 16 years searching for famous Spanish wrecks that had gone down off the Florida Keys. He proved all the naysayers wrong, after much toil and family tragedy, by discovering the *Atocha* and the *Santa Margarita*, and with them a motherlode of incredible silver bars, gold chains, chalices, ornate jewelry, and fascinating historic artifacts. Children who love to play pirate will enjoy these exhibits, but it's difficult for anyone not to be impressed by the amazing objects that were buried under the sea for so long.

Mel Fisher Maritime Museum
200 Greene St.
Key West 33040
305.294.2633
http://www.melfisher.org
Monday to Friday 8:30 a.m. to 5:00 p.m., Saturday and Sunday 9:30 a.m. to 5:00 p.m.
Adults $12.50, children $6.25
Ages: B/T, M, TW, TN

A few blocks away, you'll find the Key West Aquarium. This small attraction features local fish life found around Key West and throughout the Keys. If your children are older and have visited expansive aquariums, you may want to give this a miss. Little ones, though, will like the touch tank with its crabs, starfish, sea urchins, and other animals. Children are also permitted to touch and feed the stingrays in their pool. Guides feed their resident sharks at regular hours (11:00 a.m., 1:00 p.m., 3:00 p.m., and 4:00 p.m.). If you buy tickets online in advance, you can save approximately $2 per adult ticket and $1 per child.

DEAL

If you and your kids need a new pair of sandals, head to Front Street, take a left and go 1 block to Fitzpatrick Street, take a right and you'll find yourself at Kino Sandal Factory. The shoes—only available in Key West—are flat, simply designed thong or cross-strap sandals. The price is right, too: children's sandals cost $11 and adult shoes are $13 to $16. The family-run Kino Sandal Factory is a not-so-well-kept secret among in-the-know travelers. 107 Fitzpatrick St., 305.294.5044, http://www.kinosandals.com.

From Kino's head down to Greene Street, and then over 1 block to Key West's main drag, Duval Street. Here you'll find souvenir shops, restaurants, and, of course, the bars. Louche and charmingly disreputable-looking bars are part of Key West's claim to fame; if you ever return to the island without your children, you might want to investigate the Green Parrot Bar, the Hog's Breath Saloon, Captain Tony's, and the Bull and Whistle. In the meantime, Sloppy Joe's stands out as the most touristy and child-friendly (particularly during the day).

Sloppy Joe's can seem loud, noisy, and cavernous; it also works hard to promote its Hemingway connection. Sloppy Joe's claims to have been writer Ernest Hemingway's main watering hole in Key West. In fact, the Hemingway myth is so vital for business that its owners recently sued nearby Captain Tony's—because of its sign "The First and Original Sloppy Joe's 1933–1937." (According to biographer Paul Hendrickson, Hemingway's pal "Sloppy Joe" Russell originally opened his bar on Greene Street in the exact place where Captain Tony's now stands. It had space for dancing and was called the Silver Slipper. Hendrickson reports that in 1934 Russell—whom Hem liked to call Josie Grunts—renamed the bar "Sloppy Joe's." Later, Russell moved the joint to Duval Street, where today it continues to do a furious business . . . under corporate management. All this proves how seriously Key West takes its drinking.)

To see what all the fuss is about, you can take your family to Sloppy Joe's for lunch. The fare is straightforward, with chicken fingers, fish sandwiches, conch fritters, and pizza. Some parents may want to indulge in a rum runner or daiquiri. Live music is usually scheduled for 12:00 noon. Next door, Sloppy Joe's shop sells shot glasses, hats, totes, and the quintessential Key West souvenir, a Sloppy Joe's T-shirt depicting a bearded "Papa" Hemingway. 201 Duval St., 305.294.5717, http://www.sloppyjoes.com.

♀ INSIDE SCOOP

If Sloppy Joe's doesn't look like your thing, locals' favorite and oldest restaurant in town Pepe's Cafe is located about ⁴⁄₁₀ of a mile away. Walk on Duval from Greene to Caroline Street, then head east approximately 4 blocks. Pepe's is a funky restaurant and bar housed in a charmingly aged wooden building, with some outdoor seating; they serve breakfast, lunch, and dinner. For lunch a grilled cheese costs $6.25 and a fish sandwich is $11; the New York strip steak is $18.60. At dinnertime the prices go up, and the focus is more on steaks, with a few sandwiches. The ingredients are good, and most people love their American comfort food. Every Thursday night there's Thanksgiving dinner. 806 Caroline St., 305.294.7192, http://www.pepescafe.net. (Another option if you're not hungry just yet: wait to have lunch at Blue Heaven, a few blocks from the Ernest Hemingway Home. See directions below.)

About 2 blocks from Sloppy Joe's at 12 Duval Street (toward the water) is a CVS Pharmacy, in case you need sun protection, bottled water, or baby supplies (305.294.6337).

From Sloppy Joe's it is just a short walk to Front Street, where you can buy tickets for the Conch Tour Train. Painted red and black, with a Lilliputian "locomotive" pulling the open cars, the Conch Train is neither conch nor train. In reality it is a disguised truck pulling a series of linked trailers with seats, but let's not spoil its kitschy magic. The Conch Tour Train—for kids who aren't train experts—will certainly *look* like a train, and the loudspeaker that belts out Key West anecdotes, tall tales, and even true facts will ensure that everyone in town knows you're coming. There are 3 stops; the 2nd stop, at Truval Village (1007 Duval St.), gets you close to the Ernest Hemingway Home. You are free to get off, see the sights, and catch a later Conch Train.

For those who are by nature more inclined to subtlety, there's the City View Trolley Tour. Its handsome, vintage-style trolleys will lend your sightseeing a slightly more dignified air. The tour's 8 stops allow you to get on and get off at several different attractions. Nevertheless, the trolley is not actually a trolley; it is a bus designed to look like a trolley. Adult tickets cost $21 or $19 if bought online, and children under 12 years are free (http://www. cityviewtrolleys.com or 305.294.0644). The trolley's first stop is at 105 Whitehead Street, not far from the Key West Aquarium and Mel Fisher Maritime Museum.

〰〰〰〰〰〰〰〰〰〰〰〰〰〰〰〰〰〰

Conch Tour Train
201 Front St.
Key West 33040
888.916.8687
http://www.conchtourtrain.com
Adults $30.45 ($27.41 if purchased online), children 12 and under
  ride free

〰〰〰〰〰〰〰〰〰〰〰〰〰〰〰〰〰〰

Ernest Hemingway was not only one of America's most influential writers and a Nobel Prize recipient, he was also a Key West legend. He moved here with his wife Pauline and bought a large, gracious home where he wrote *To Have and Have Not* and *Green Hills of Africa*. The 1851 house is constructed of coral rock and Georgia pine; it has iron railings upstairs, which make it look more typical of New Orleans' French Quarter than Key West. Tours of the Ernest Hemingway Home are informative and entertaining; there are plenty of amusing anecdotes about the house and its owner. If your children don't know who Hemingway was, this experience will introduce them to him and probably create an interest in his work. Smaller kids will be curious about his collection of 6-toed cats, whose descendants still have the run of the property. Despite its size, the house feels unpretentious, so that you can almost imagine Hem himself banging through the door in shorts and sandals after a long, hard day's fishing.

The Ernest Hemingway Home and Museum
907 Whitehead St.
Key West 33040
305.294.1575
http://www.hemingwayhome.com
Adults $13, children $6, children 5 and under free
9:00 a.m. to 5:00 p.m., 7 days a week
Ages: M, TW, TN

If you've eschewed the noise of Sloppy Joe's and the funky cool of Pepe's, and need a place for lunch, head about a block up to Petronia Street, then go a long block west to Thomas Street. Since it opened decades ago, Blue Heaven (formerly Ricky's Blue Heaven) Restaurant has transformed from a dusty, rambling joint (with chickens) to a somewhat more touristy, professionally run establishment (with chickens). Scrumptious pancakes for breakfast; grilled cheese and grouper sandwiches for lunch; and barbecue shrimp and seafood specials at dinner. At times the wait for a table gets irksome. 729 Thomas St., Key West 33040, 305.296.8666, http://www.blueheavenkw.com.

Children old enough to climb 88 steps of an iron staircase may be fascinated by the Key West Lighthouse and Keeper's Quarters Museum, located close to the Ernest Hemingway Home on Whitehead Street. The educational experience shows children what it was like to run a lighthouse, with its huge Fresnel lens, instruments, maps, and artifacts, along with the restored keeper's house. The lighthouse dates from 1886 and encompasses important Keys' history.

Key West Lighthouse and Keeper's Quarters Museum
938 Whitehead St.
Key West 33040
305.294.0012
http://www.kwahs.com
Adults $10, children $6, children under 6 free
9:30 a.m. to 4:30 p.m., 7 days a week
Ages: M, TW, TN

Once you leave the Key West Lighthouse, you can catch a ride with the Conch Tour Train at Truval Village on Duval Street. Or, if your children are up for a walk, you can head further up Duval on foot to the Key West Butterfly and Nature Conservatory. (From the lighthouse this is approximately 7/10 of a mile.) In the conservatory there are hundreds of butterflies, which have been hatched (not collected in the wild) and also tropical birds and flowers. The Learning Center shows a 15-minute film and has exhibits about butterfly anatomy and migration. The gift shop, with its many trinkets, books, and souvenirs, is an enticing place to round out your visit.

Key West Butterfly and Nature Conservatory
1316 Duval St.
Key West 33040
305.296.2988

http://www.keywestbutterfly.com
Adults $12, children (4–12) $8.50, children under 3 free
9:00 a.m. to 5:00 p.m., 7 days a week
Ages: B/T, M, TW, TN

♀ INSIDE SCOOP

One of the most inexpensive souvenirs you can buy in the Keys
is bottled key lime juice. Key lime pie is shockingly easy to make.
Take a premade graham cracker crust from the grocery store, and
following the recipe from your key lime juice bottle, add 3 ingredients: key lime juice, sweetened condensed milk, and egg yolks.
You cook that sucker and then refrigerate. Top or don't top the pie
with fresh (not store bought) whipped cream, depending on your
taste, and presto! You have a deliciously authentic, sweet-and-tart
Florida Keys masterpiece.

The Conch Train's final stop is at Flagler Station Oversea Railway Historeum, a small museum dedicated to the railroad built
by industrialist Henry Flagler. This line first connected the Keys
to one another and to the mainland. Your train ticket gets you
free admission. Here you see a reconstruction of the railroad
terminus and can also watch 3 short films about this incredible
engineering feat. Children can walk inside a railroad car and see
memorabilia (Flagler Station, 901 Caroline St.).

Right near the Conch Train's final stop is the Half Shell Raw
Bar, a restaurant on the marina known for its fresh seafood.
Whether you are stopping in for dessert or for an early dinner
before returning to Miami, Half Shell Raw Bar is a relaxed place
to get a bite. Menu items include shrimp, steamed clams, oysters, fish and chips baskets, sandwiches, and fish dinners that
are simply but well prepared. There is no pretension here: just
picnic tables, license plates nailed to the walls, good seafood, and
one of the best key lime pies around. 231 Margaret St., Key West
33040, 305.294.7496, http://www.halfshellrawbar.com.

There's a bit of a trek from Half Shell Raw Bar to Mallory Square to catch the bus, so give yourselves time. (Or hail a taxi or an expensive Pedicab and take a ride.) Depending on the time of year and the time of the sunset, you may or may not be able to witness some of the performers and vendors who crowd Mallory Square before the sun oozes into the horizon in a burst of violet and pink glory. This is tourist central, with some fun sights for kids to see before you board the bus (or get into the car) for the ride back north. Certainly, the colorful characters and the crafts for sale make it difficult to say good-bye to this unique island.

Key West is a destination that many vacationers return to again and again, just like Miami. There will be plenty of sights to see and museums to visit when you return: the Harry S. Truman Little White House, the Shipwreck Treasures Museum, the Audubon House, the Eco-Discovery Center, and the USCGC Ingham Memorial Museum, not to mention snorkeling and sunset trips. Plus, there are the Dry Tortugas and historic Fort Jefferson to reach by boat or plane. The activities are far too varied to fit into a single day-trip, but don't let that discourage you from visiting the island. Time spent in the parallel universe that is the Florida Keys will give you the chance to appreciate beautiful vistas of Caribbean water, appealing architecture, delicious food, and an unpretentious, unconventional way of life. This part of southern Florida, along with the Everglades, makes for a terrific counterpoint to the metropolitan attractions you'll find in the ever-happening, ever cool city of Miami.

Acknowledgments

My sincere thanks go to:

Excellent editors Sian Hunter and Marthe Walters, along with
Meredith Morris-Babb, Shannon McCarthy, Larry Leshan,
Romi Gutierrez, Ale Gasso, Rachel Doll, and the terrific pro-
fessionals at the University Press of Florida,
Mapmaker Tracy Ellen Smith and copy editor Beth Detwiler,
Inspirational workshop magician Connie May Fowler,
Gifted novelist and Miami native Susanna Daniel,
Writers Martha Otis, Rich McKee, and Lisa Hartz for generous
feedback and advice, particularly Martha's Miami expertise,
Editor Glenn Harper for Miami assignments in *Sculpture*,
Keys historian Brad Bertelli for incisive critiques and kind
encouragement,
Miami friends who have explored the city with us: Joanna,
Rose, Mia, Rafaela, Sam, Bruno, Sophia, Laura, Faye, Mar-
tha, Serena, Ben, Carrie, Evy, and JoJo (especially Joanna
and Carrie for thoughtful suggestions on the manuscript),
Dear out-of-town friends who joined us for Miami expeditions:
Maggie, Liz, Brian, Maureen, Nora, Milner, Kathryn, Scott,
and June,
My wonderful parents, Ann and Dallas, for all the amazing
travels and adventures they took me on as a child,
Iris, for bringing me so much happiness,
And Zickie, for his unflagging optimism, support, and love.

Notes

Chapter 2. A Brief History of Miami

13   *In 1513, Spanish explorer*: Parks and Bush, 2.

13   *The consequence of disease*: Parks and Bush, 3.

14   *As a result of the nautical dangers*: Parks, 10.

14   *In 1838 Fort Dallas*: Muir, 16.

14   *William and Mary Brickell ran*: Muir, 7.

14   *The year 1896 was momentous*: Muir, 57.

16   *John Collins for whom Collins Avenue*: Muir, 99.

16   *Fisher even imported*: Muir, 102.

16   *Developers, entrepreneurs, and ordinary people*: Muir, 131.

16   *When the Great Depression seized*: Parks, 13.

16   *When the United States entered World War II*: Parks and Bush, 101.

17   *In 1979, 4 white police officers*: Parks and Bush, 178.

17   *In a few months almost 125,000*: Parks and Bush, 175.

18   *In the later 1990s*: Wisckol.

Chapter 3. Key Biscayne

23   *A schooner from the northeast*: Blank, 95.

Chapter 4. Coconut Grove

48   *Member Mary Barr Munroe*: Parks and Bennett, 25.

Chapter 5. South Beach

60   *Due to a minor but insurmountable hitch*: Nash, 29.

60   *He had better luck starting in*: Stofik, 8.

60   *Then Collins' family had a brainstorm*: Stofik, 9.

61   *Collins and his son-in-law Thomas Pancoast*: Stofik, 10.

Chapter 6. Mid-Beach and Beyond

94   *Lapidus himself wore a bow tie*: Nash, 70.

96   *"People want architecture . . ."*: Nash, 70.

96   *He not only pioneered MiMo*: Nash, 41–2, 71.

Chapter 7. Coral Gables and Little Havana

105   *"Coral Gables" was originally*: Uguccioni, 100.

Chapter 8. Southern Miami

126   *Decades ago, a place called the Rare Bird Farm*: Pranty, 146.

126   *But in the 1960s*: Pranty, 146.

Chapter 9. Downtown

139   *In return the Seminoles*: Parks, 13.

151   *Architect Harold Hastings Mundy*: Gordon, 191.

152   *Before the 1961 Bay of Pigs*: Gordon, 194.

Chapter 10. Wynwood and the Design District

157   *Sculptor Pepe Mar remembers*: Albritton, 56.

163   *The Moore Building originally*: Alvarado.

167   *Its gorgeous blue-and-white tile murals*: Nash, 115.

167   *At 2919 Biscayne*: Nash, 117.

167   *Edwin Reeder designed the Shalimar Motel*: Nash, 97.

Chapter 11. Further Afield

194   *Later, Russell moved the joint*: Hendrickson, 150.

196   *The 1851 house is constructed*: Hendrickson, 94.

Bibliography

Albritton, Laura. "Dressing Up Sculpture: An Interview with Pepe Mar." *Sculpture* (April 2013): 52–57.

Alvarado, Francisco. "Miami Design District Crime Challenges $312 Million Luxury Overhaul." *Miami New Times*, March 7, 2013. http://www.miaminewtimes.com (accessed May 29, 2013).

Blank, Joan Gill. "Key Biscayne." *Miami's Historic Neighborhoods*. Edited by Becky Roper Matkov, 94–99. San Antonio, Tex.: Historical Publishing Network, 2001.

Gordon, Elsbeth. *Heart and Soul of Florida: Sacred Sites and Historic Architecture*. Gainesville: University Press of Florida, 2013.

Hendrickson, Paul. *Hemingway's Boat*. New York: Alfred A. Knopf, 2011.

Muir, Helen. *Miami, U.S.A.* Gainesville: University Press of Florida, 2000.

Nash, Eric P., and Randall C. Robinson, Jr. *MiMo: Miami Modern Revealed.* San Francisco: Chronicle Books, 2004.

Parks, Arva Moore. "History Is Where You Find It." *Miami's Historic Neighborhoods*. Edited by Becky Roper Matkov, 10–14. San Antonio, Tex.: Historical Publishing Network, 2001.

Parks, Arva Moore, and Bo Bennett. *Images of America: Coconut Grove.* Charleston, S.C.: Arcadia Publishing, 2010.

Parks, Arva Moore, and Gregory W. Bush. *Miami: The American Crossroad.* Coral Gables, Fla.: Institute for Public History, 1996.

Pranty, Bill. "Status and Current Range of Red-Whiskered Bulbuls." *Florida Field Naturalist* 38, no. 4 (2010): 146–49.

Stofik, M. Barron. *Saving South Beach.* Gainesville: University Press of Florida, 2005.

Uguccioni, Ellen J. "Coral Gables." In *Miami's Historic Neighborhoods.* Edited by Becky Roper Matkov, 100–105. San Antonio, Tex.: Historical Publishing Network, 2001.

Wisckol, Martin. "Miami's Debt Rating Takes Plunge." *Sun-Sentinel*, November 30, 1996. http://www.sunsentinel.com (accessed February 23, 2013).

Index

LAURA ALBRITTON is a writer and Florida native. Her work has been published in the *Miami Herald*, the *Houston Chronicle*, *Harvard Review*, *Sculpture* magazine, and the *Times Literary Supplement*. Her award-winning short fiction has appeared in more than 20 literary journals. She lives in Miami with her husband and daughter.

The University Press of Florida is the scholarly publishing agency for the State University System of Florida, comprising Florida A&M University, Florida Atlantic University, Florida Gulf Coast University, Florida International University, Florida State University, New College of Florida, University of Central Florida, University of Florida, University of North Florida, University of South Florida, and University of West Florida.